Deceived by Darkness

Authors

Jerald Joersz, Reynold Kremer, Max Murphy, Robert Smith, and Jesse Yow

Editors

Mark Sengele, Henry Gerike

Your comments and suggestions concerning this material are appreciated. Please write the Editor of Youth Materials, Concordia Publishing House, 3558 S. Jefferson Avenue, St. Louis, MO 63118-3968.

This publication is also available in braille and in large type for the visually impaired. Call 1-800-433-3954, or write to Library for the Blind, 1333 S. Kirkwood Rd., St. Louis, MO 63122-7295.

Contents

Introduction

About *Deceived by Darkness*

"This is the verdict: Light has come into the world, but men loved darkness instead of light because their deeds were evil. Everyone who does evil hates the light, and will not come into the light for fear that his deeds will be exposed" (John 3:19–20).

In this present age of religious tolerance a great variety of formerly counter-cultural religious groups have become more mainstream. This study seeks to expose the deeds of these darker religious practices in the light of the Word of God.

Deceived by Darkness casts the light of the Word on seven different religious groups or practices. Our goal is not to increase curious interest in any of these false practices or to somehow glorify them. Rather we desire to glorify Christ who is the Light of the World, the Victorious One over the eternal dangers of darkness.

The subjects and Bible studies in this book are appropriate for high school youth and adults. For those who might have opportunity to combine youth and adults in an intergenerational setting, some study suggestions are given later in this introduction.

Why This Study?

Fascination with occultic practices is at an all-time high. Popular media has normalized and glamorized much of what was once considered dark, secret, and dangerous. Today's young people are caught in a world that tells them all beliefs should be tolerated. Ironically, Christianity's exclusive beliefs and intolerance of false teaching are not tolerated by many people in this "open-minded" world. A study like this is not popular.

At the same time researchers are telling us that spiritual searching and expression are at an all-time high for youth. Unfortunately, much of that spirituality follows a smorgasbord approach to faith, borrowing bits and pieces from a variety of religious practices and traditions. Young people need to hear the truth that salvation is found only through the work of Christ on the cross of Calvary.

Preparing to Teach

Each of the eight studies in this book follows a similar format; the lesson focus, objectives, and a simple outline of the study are provided at the beginning of each lesson. The introductory statements are followed by detailed leader's directions and reproducible participant resource pages. A glossary of terms used in the lessons can be found at the back of the book.

For each class session the leader should make enough copies of the resource pages for the class participants. Resource pages should be distributed at the time indicated in the leader's directions.

Basic class supplies include pens or pencils for each student, blank paper, and a chalkboard or equivalent (whiteboard, newsprint pad and easel) with appropriate markers or chalk. Encourage participants to bring along their own Bibles. Keep a supply of Bibles on hand for visitors or students who do not bring their own. The lesson outline suggests supplies needed for each section of the lesson.

Each study is completely outlined for the leader, including suggested lengths of time for each portion of the study. The suggested times total 50 to 60 minutes. In some cases, depending on class participation, it may be necessary to use additional time or to omit portions of the lesson. Some lessons also contain ideas for extending the lesson or for alternative activities within the lesson.

Leader's directions also suggest when to have students work together as a whole group or as smaller breakout groups of two to four students. These breakout directions are designed to facilitate more intimate discussion of the material. If your numbers are small, you may choose to ignore these breakout suggestions. In some cases the leader may wish to have the whole group discuss instead of discussing in the smaller breakout groups.

Most of us do well when there are no surprises. Leaders are encouraged to review each lesson fully, well in advance of its presentation. Materials can then be tailored to your students' preferences as well as your own.

Adapting These Studies

It is not required that you use all eight lessons in this study, or that you use them in the order they appear. You may wish to use the lessons independently as students raise questions or interest concerning one of the subjects. You may wish to skip the study of "Real Religion," save it for use at the end of the series, or use it both to begin and conclude the series. You may wish to adapt one or more lessons for a retreat or lock-in format. It may be necessary to supply additional questions or discussion for use by your group. In some cases it may be desirable to split lessons and use them over more than one session. Such adaptations are appropriate, perhaps even necessary, for the best possible results.

Adults and youth—even parents and their teenagers—can study these lessons together. While such classes are rare in most churches, there are certain benefits to discussing matters of faith in intergenerational groups. This is especially true when addressing religious movements that can easily draw young people away from the true God.

It is necessary to be sensitive to the needs of youth and adults when leading intergenerational groups.

Provide leadership opportunities for young people and adults. Let adults and youth share reading responsibilities, breakout group leadership tasks, and response reporting duties.

Facilitate interaction. Unless they have had opportunity to study together before, some youth and adults may be reluctant initially to share answers with one another. Use opening group questions and sharing time to level the playing field for youth and adults.

Set a comfort level. Help groups understand that not everyone will want to share, read aloud for the group, or answer every question. Help groups work toward a level of trust with one another.

Resources

Internet resources abound on the subjects found in these studies. Any number of search engines will facilitate further study. A number of Web sites are mentioned within the lessons. Caution should be observed since much of the information found on the World Wide Web is not verifiable. Exercise spiritual discernment as you browse, testing information against the truth of God's Word.

At the end of each lesson there are resources listed that provide further information on the lesson topic. Each resource listed is marked with a symbol to indicate confidence or concerns about that resource.

Indicates those resources that are appropriate for general use. The author or publisher is considered a reliable source.

👁 Indicates resources that should be used or viewed with caution.

🕷 Indicates resources that may be inappropriate for general use by students.

📚 Jim Watkins, *The Why Files—Is There Really Life After Death?* (St. Louis: Concordia Publishing House, 2001)

📚 Jim Watkins, *The Why Files—Are There Really Ghosts?* (St. Louis: Concordia Publishing House, 2001)

📚 *One God, Many gods—Bible Studies for Postmodern Teens* (St. Louis: Concordia Publishing House, 1998)

1

Real Religion and Virtual Religion: Faith is Built on Christ the Rock

Lesson Focus

At first glance, many of the practices we will study do not appear religious. Yet they fill a spiritual void and may contain certain rituals and practices that are similar to organized religions. To understand these practices, we need to understand why people do them. To understand people who practice pagan, occultic, New Age, or shamanistic techniques or follow the doctrines that support them, we need to know what is in the very center of the heart—theirs and ours.

Objectives

By the power of the Holy Spirit, the participants, through the study of God's Word, will

> **1.** learn how to study a religious system, using the basic elements of the Christian faith as a foundation for comparison;
>
> **2.** identify why occultic practices should be considered religious in nature, belonging to a false god;
>
> **3.** thank God for His grace in giving faith to them, feel compassion for the lost, and grow in a desire to witness to believers caught in false religions.

Activity	Time Suggested	Materials Needed
Prayer The Survey Says ...	2 minutes 5–7 minutes	Newsprint and markers, Copies of Resource Page 1A
Religion Begins in the Heart	15 minutes	Copies of Resource Page 1A, Bibles
The Threefold Seduction of the Dark Side	10 minutes	Copies of Resource Page 1B, Bibles
What Does God Think about Other Religions?	15 minutes	Copies of Resource Page 1C, Bibles
Closing Prayer	5 minutes	None

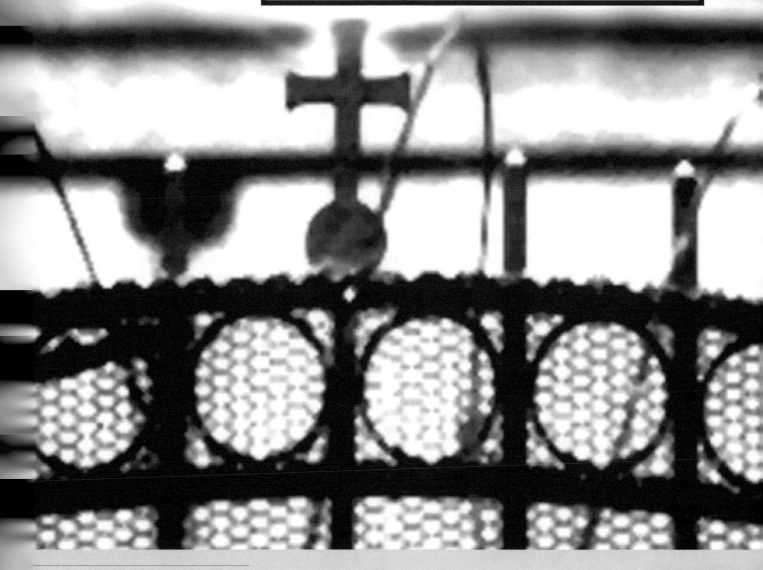

Opening Prayer (2 minutes)

Begin with a prayer: "Heavenly Father, when we were baptized, Your Holy Spirit gave us faith to trust Your Son for salvation. Through faithful parents, teachers, and pastors, You have caused that faith to grow. By the study of Your holy Word, You have deepened our knowledge of Your world and this precious trust in You. Grant that we may better understand why some people are drawn to the deceptive practices of Satan, following false systems of faith. Show us how You would have us bring the Gospel to them. This we ask in Your name and for the sake of Your Son, Jesus Christ, our Lord. Amen."

The Survey Says ... (5–7 minutes)

Tell your class that you will begin this session with a survey. Distribute copies of Resource Page 1A. Divide the class into breakout groups of two to four people. Assign each group a practice or movement to analyze from page 1A. You may allow groups to select a practice or movement they are likely to know something about. Each group should list everything they think the group believes or everything the practices are supposed to do for those who participate in them. The answers they give do not need to be correct. In fact, this session is more effective if responses are not terribly accurate. Give groups about five minutes to work. After five minutes, reassemble the whole group. Ask a volunteer from each group to list the beliefs discussed. Write them on the blackboard or newsprint for the whole class to see.

Most of the answers will likely focus on things the movement asks its followers to do. Point out how many of the benefits of the practice will be nonreligious in character, self serving, and potentially dangerous to others. If the class focused on actual teachings or the spiritual nature of an activity, praise them for perceiving the truth of the matter. The things that people do are influenced by their values and beliefs; faith is not created by the things people do.

Alternate Opening Activity

Ask the class what their non-Lutheran friends think Lutherans believe or, for a more specific example, why others think Lutherans take communion. Ask if the replies their friends give are accurate. If not, why not?

Make the transition to the lesson by saying something such as, "When it comes to spiritual things, people tend to focus on what is easy to see and understand. We remember what people do and what people say, and we remember the most visible practices of a group. Practices like yoga or martial arts may be harmless, or they may be harmful. Many people do not realize that some who are heavily involved in these activities may also have a spiritual basis in the religions behind them. The activities may be spiritual practices for those who do them. The New Age, occultic, and pagan practices we will study are no different. In fact, people often do not realize that many common activities have a religious background and connection. When we try to speak to friends who do these things, we may struggle to make much progress in witnessing to them—especially if we do not understand what they believe. In this class we will learn how to study other religions, using our Lutheran Christian faith as a basis and framework for comparison."

Throughout this book the words "God" and "god" will appear. When using the uppercase "God," we refer to the one true God. The lowercase "god" refers to any number of false gods.

Religion Begins in the Heart (15 minutes)

Have students read the quote from Martin Luther from Resource Page 1A. Ask students to share what they think this quote means. Explain to students that a person's faith begins with the one central belief they value most highly in their heart. Like a house built on a foundation, a person's life is built upon this core value. Everything people do proceeds from this belief. Upon this foundation of core values is built the "basement" of other things a person believes to be true. Some decisions and experiences are made from this solid living area. On this basement rests the "floors" and "walls" that come from a person's experiences and training. Finally, the "windows" and "interior"—how a person acts and lives—are built on this shell. The culture in which the person lives can be compared to the soil that surrounds the foundation and basement. If a man challenges things on the upstairs level but never looks at the foundation, he will not critically examine his religion or evaluate his practices. If his faith is built on one or more false premises, the whole building is weak and will eventually fall—on the Last Day, if not sooner.

Explain that to understand why people behave the way they do, we need to understand their core values, their beliefs, and the faith in their heart. The rest of the section provides the students with tools to do a values/beliefs/faith analysis. Assign breakout groups one of the four principles of a religion. Ask students to read the selected Bible verses and then write what that principle would be for the Lutheran church. After students have finished their work, have them share with the whole group. It may be helpful to share some of the following information concerning each principle:

Central Teaching—what a religion is built around. You may compare the central teaching of a religion to a closet. All the teachings of a religion can be put together by hanging them on the rack of this central teaching. For Lutheranism, the central teaching is "salvation by grace through faith for Christ's sake alone." We can better understand other teachings, such as Law and Gospel, the Sacraments, and worship, by explaining them in terms of this teaching.

Source of Authority—that which forms or shapes a religion. What is the source of teaching, or the authority, the leaders use to guide the beliefs of the church? Most religions refer their believers to a series of teachers, sacred texts, or other authorities. In practice, most religions depend upon one or just a few sources. Many of them are written. These texts form or shape the religion's teachings. For Lutheranism, the Bible—God's Word—is the source of authority. God's Word, in turn, is interpreted and explained by our written creeds and confessions that shape our teachings and practice.

Worldview—how a religion organizes the world. A worldview describes who God, gods, or spiritual beings are; how people relate to them; how people relate to one another; and how people relate to the world around them. For Lutherans, God is three persons in one: Father, Son, and Holy Spirit. The Father is the Creator of the world. Through the Son's death on the cross, the debt of the world's sin was paid for all people. By the work of the Holy Spirit, through Word and Sacraments, faith is created and sustained so believers are children of God and heirs to eternal life. Fellow believers are brothers and sisters in Christ, organized into churches by their common faith. Believers—by the Holy Spirit's power—serve God by sharing the Gospel, praising God, serving others, and taking care of God's world. A person's worldview guides decisions and forms one's plan for action.

Salvation History— how the world got this way and what can be done to change it. For most non-Christian religions, people must do something to make life better now and for their afterlife. Many times a god or spiritual beings are involved. Christian salvation history tells the story of how God acted to save believers. For Lutherans, salvation history begins before creation and moves through the creation and the fall to the coming of Christ. All of the Scriptures present a unified view of salvation history. It culminates with the life, death, resurrection, and ascension of Jesus. It moves through the history of God's Church to the end of time. It concludes in eternity, where God will destroy sin, death, and the power of the devil and will live with His children forever in heaven.

The Threefold Seduction of the Dark Side (10 minutes)

Ultimately, most false religions prey upon three common issues that face each person—guilt, fear, and power. Every person, even nonbelievers, deals with guilt—whether it is genuine guilt over sin or regret over mistakes. Many false religions believe that guilt can be eliminated by performing some greater good. Most people at one time or another deal with fear—ultimately the fear of death. Many false religions make false promises or explain the afterlife to take away a person's fear. The third issue people struggle with is a desire for power and control in the midst of weakness and insignificance. Most people wish they had more control over things in life. Most false religions offer a kind of power or control, offering personal gain for those who follow their religious path. These promises include supernatural power to those who use a certain mantra, potion, routine, or practice.

Distribute copies of Resource Page 1B to each student. Have students look up God's answers to each of these three concerns. Guilt is taken away by the mercy and grace of God, through Jesus Christ, who paid the price for our sin. Fear is diminished by the promises of God, especially the promises of God's protection and perfect peace. God's power is shown in the work of the Holy Spirit as the Spirit changes lives from the inside out. Supernatural miracles also happen, but they are not the goal of the Christian's life. There are only two sources of supernatural power: God and Satan. If a supernatural event ever occurs, we should determine its source of power. If the event isn't in accordance with God's power, love, and forgiveness for His children, and it doesn't make us say, "Wow" and sing God's praises, and it doesn't tie in to the Great Commission, then it probably is not a work of God.*

*A note about the last statement: The Gospel of John uses a term for miracle that literally means "sign." Matthew, Mark, and Luke frequently use a term that means "something that makes me marvel." Just before ascending into heaven,

Jesus said, "All power in heaven and on earth has been given to Me, therefore go and make disciples" (Matthew 28: 18-19).

What Does God Think about Other Religions?

(15 minutes)

Distribute copies of Resource Page 1C. You may wish to have each breakout group take one section and report to the larger group a summary of the Scripture verses listed for each section. If time allows, you may choose to have the whole group work through all of the verses together with student volunteers reading selected verses aloud.

The first section explores the question of other gods. Exodus 20 is the text of the First Commandment. God adds two examples of what the First Commandment forbids. Make sure the class understands that God commands that we have only one God and warns that to do otherwise invites God's curse. Isaiah 45 emphasizes that there are no other gods. Paul's Agora sermon (Acts 17) argues that all gods beyond ours are not real at all.

The second section looks at what the Scripture says about other religions. In Matthew 7, Jesus warns against false christs that deceive people into thinking they can serve God while taking an easy road to salvation. Later, in Matthew 7:24-27, Jesus counsels us to build on the solid foundation of His Word. In Romans 1, Paul makes his case against false gods and reveals God's punishment for people's disobedience. In Galatians, Paul points out that those who worship other gods become slaves to them. Christ has come to free us from this slavery. In Colossians, Paul warns us against being captured by false philosophies and works-based spiritual schemes. In 2 Timothy, Paul exhorts young Pastor Timothy to preach God's Word in the face of popular religious movements and teachers who tell people what they want to hear. In 2 Peter, the apostle Peter warns about destructive heresies in the church. Together, these passages show us that other religions are false and threaten our salvation. In the John passage, Jesus points out that salvation comes from following Him and no one else.

At this point, the class may come to the conclusion that God hates non-Christians. However, the next section shows that God really loves them and sent Jesus to save everyone. Ezekiel records God's promise to seek and to gather people, even the lost ones, from the ends of the earth. He will shepherd them like a good shepherd. In Matthew, we learn that Jesus has compassion on the lost and wants us to pray for workers in His harvest field. In Luke, Jesus gives us His mission statement: to seek and to save the lost. Finally, in the John passage, we learn how much God loves the world.

The final section asks how we should relate to those who follow false gods. God tells us in Isaiah that believers are His witnesses, sent to tell others the truth about Him. In Matthew 28, Jesus sends out His Church to make more disciples by sharing Christ's message with all people, by baptizing them, and by teaching them everything God has commanded. In Acts 1, Jesus expands on this by telling His disciples to start at home and then move out to the ends of the world. In 1 Peter, the apostle Peter tells us always to be ready to reply gently and respectfully to those who ask about the faith. Finally, Jude tells us to work for the salvation of unbelievers and to snatch them from the fires of eternal hell.

Closing Prayer (5 minutes)

Close the session with a prayer: "Dear Jesus, You came to seek and save the lost. Help us to understand the faith of others and, by Your grace, bless our witness to them. By Your Holy Spirit bring them to faith and build their lives on the solid rock of faith in You, who with the Father and the Spirit are one God, now and forever. Amen."

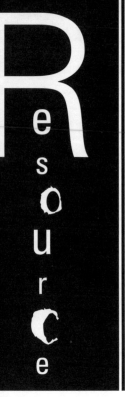

The Survey Says ...

What do each of the following groups do—what do they teach or practice?

Wicca/Covens

Church of Satan

Voodoo

Mysticism

Vampire Cults

Fortune Tellers/Mediums

Religion Begins in the Heart

"A 'god' is the term for that to which we are to look for all good and in which we are to find refuge in all need. Therefore, to have a god is nothing else than to trust and believe in that one with your whole heart. As I have often said, it is trust and faith of the heart alone that make both God and an idol" (Martin Luther, Large Catechism in *The Book of Concord*, First Commandment, Paragraph 2).

Central Teaching—what a religion is built around. **Ephesians 2:8–10; Romans 1:16–17; 5:1–10**

Source of Authority—forms or shapes a religion. **2 Timothy 3:15–17; 1 Thessalonians 2:13**

Worldview—how a religion sees the world. **Matthew 7:24–27; 12:33–35; 15:1–20**

Salvation History—how the world got this way and what God is doing about it. **John 1:1–18**

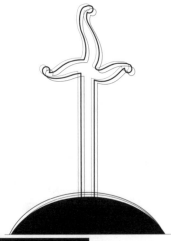

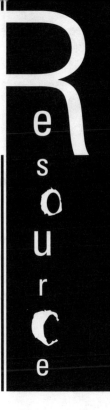

The Threefold Seduction of the Dark Side

Most dark spiritual forces prey upon three human weaknesses: guilt, fear, and weakness/powerlessness. What does God provide as the genuine answer when any of these three concerns arise?

Guilt—   **Romans 5:8**

Romans 6:23

Fear—   **Isaiah 26:3–4**

John 14:27

John 16:33

Power—   **2 Corinthians 4:5–18**

2 Corinthians 12:7–10

2 Thessalonians 2:5–17

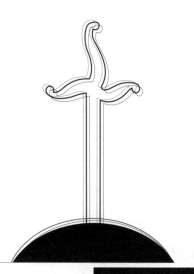

2001 Concordia Publishing House, St Louis. Reproduced by permission. Scripture: NIV®.

What Does God Think about Other Religions?

In America at the beginning of the twenty-first century, society celebrates our differences. Television, radio, and many universities teach young adults that all religions are true. The only belief considered wrong is the belief that there is only one true religion. The Scripture verses below tell us how God feels about false religions. Look up each passage and answer the questions.

Are other gods real?

Exodus 20:3–6

Isaiah 45:18–20

Acts 17:22–31

What is the truth about other religions?

Matthew 7:13–23

Romans 1:18–32

Galatians 4:8–11

Colossians 2:9–10, 18–19

2 Timothy 3:1–9

2 Peter 2:1–3

John 14:5–7

2001 Concordia Publishing House, St Louis. Reproduced by permission. Scripture: NIV®.

What is God doing about it?

Ezekiel 34:11–16

Matthew 9:36–38

Luke 19:10

John 3:16–17

How should we relate to other religions?

Isaiah 43:8–13

Matthew 28:18–20

Acts 1:8

1 Peter 3:15–16

Jude 17–23

2001 Concordia Publishing House, St Louis. Reproduced by permission. Scripture: NIV®.

Witchcraft—
falling Prey to a Power Play

Lesson Focus

Wicca is the Old English term for *witch*. Witchcraft seeks power through the worship of a pagan Ultimate Deity. Through the study of the truth of the Bible, we see that Wicca is a powerless religion. Only through the true God—Father, Son, and Holy Spirit—do we receive power for living.

Objectives

By the power of the Holy Spirit, the participants, through the study of God's Word, will

1. understand the teachings of Wicca;

2. come to see that the only true source of power for living is our eternal, triune God.

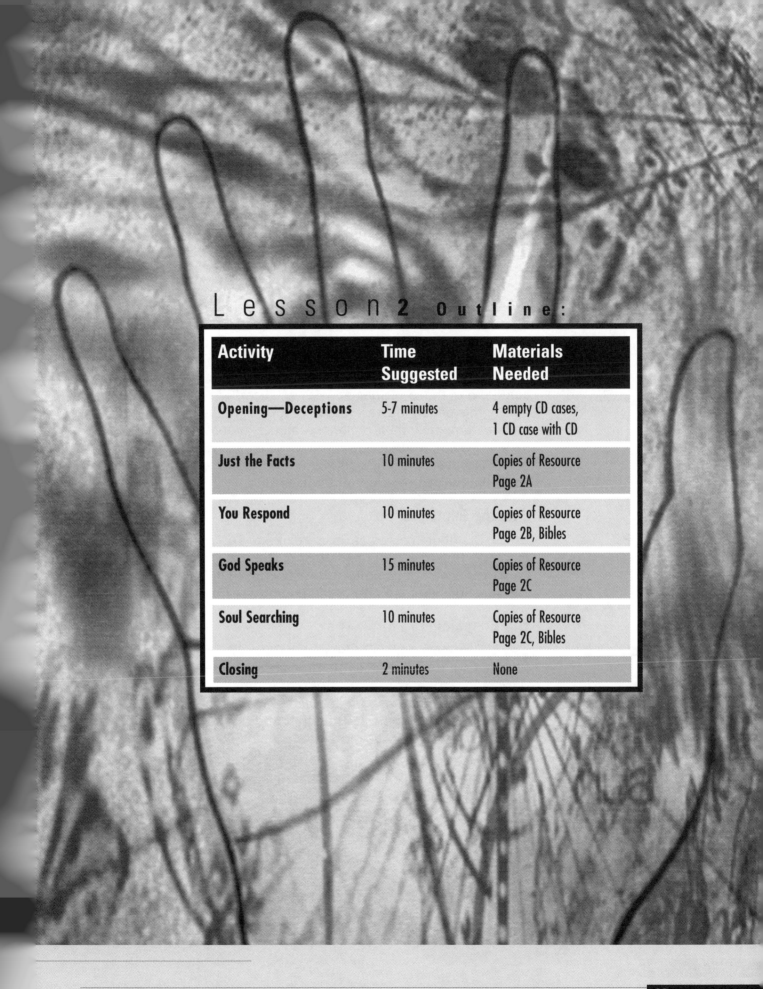

Lesson 2 Outline:

Activity	Time Suggested	Materials Needed
Opening—Deceptions	5-7 minutes	4 empty CD cases, 1 CD case with CD
Just the Facts	10 minutes	Copies of Resource Page 2A
You Respond	10 minutes	Copies of Resource Page 2B, Bibles
God Speaks	15 minutes	Copies of Resource Page 2C
Soul Searching	10 minutes	Copies of Resource Page 2C, Bibles
Closing	2 minutes	None

Opening—Deceptions (5–7 minutes)

You'll need five CD cases—only one containing a CD, the other four empty. Set the five boxes on a desk and say to students, "One of these CD cases contains a CD, the other four do not. Your assignment is to figure out how you can discover which has the CD without opening them up and peeking inside. What methods would you use to find the real one? On the surface, some deceptions look very inviting. How can you learn to tell the difference?" Give students time to share their insights.

Because of the frightening nature of this subject, it cannot be emphasized enough that the dangers of dabbling in witchcraft are real. Everything connected with witchcraft is despised by God (see Martin Luther, The Large Catechism in *The Book of Concord*, Second Commandment). The purpose of this lesson is not to spur curiosity, but to show the sad condition of those connected with witchcraft. In order not to glorify this pagan lifestyle, little mention is made of their nude ceremonies, their pagan worship of nature, their feminist viewpoint, or their hatred of Christianity. Their reference books are filled with rites and ceremonies, prayers, and practices that make a mockery of the true God.

Just the Facts (10 minutes)

Distribute copies of Resource Page 2A. Read through this page together with the students. Discuss any questions they may have at this time. You may want to delay answering questions that are addressed later in the study.

You Respond (10 minutes)

Distribute copies of Resource Page 2B. This section contains a number of statements concerning the teachings of Wicca. Ask students to work alone or in small breakout groups to read and respond to each of the statements. After a few minutes call the class together and discuss their responses. Suggested responses are as follows:

Emphasize the danger of dabbling in anything connected with the occult. Such dabbling will produce dangerous consequences sooner or later.

The Scriptures clearly show us how to tell if a church is the true church (see Romans 8:9; Ephesians 2:20; 2 Timothy 4:3; 1 John 4:1). The Bible clearly tells us that hell is a real place (see Matthew 5:29–30; 2 Peter 2:4).

"Just as man is destined to die once, and after that to face judgment" (Hebrews 9:27). Hebrews 9:27 refutes all New Age beliefs about reincarnation.

If in Scripture, a perfect God, Judgment Day, and heaven and hell are removed from the picture, humans are left to have free moral reign with no accountability whatsoever.

God Speaks (15 minutes)

Distribute copies of Resource Page 2C. Have students use their breakout groups to look up and discuss each of the Bible verses listed for this section. The following is a quick summary of practices mentioned in each verse:

Ezekiel 13:23: **DIVINATION** (using the occult to tell the past, present, or future with things such as tarot cards, crystal balls, or astrology)

Exodus 8:19: **MAGICIANS** (using supernatural powers to bring about special effects—sometimes called magick to distinguish it from theater magic)

Isaiah 8:19: **MEDIUMS AND SPIRITISTS** (those who make contact with the dead or other spirits—their actions are sometimes referred to as channeling)

Isaiah 47:9: **SORCERY** (see magicians)

Micah 5:12: **WITCHCRAFT** (see magicians)

God's Word speaks clearly about those who are involved in these practices:

Deuteronomy 18:10–13: God demands that these detestable practices be driven out and that we become blameless in His sight.

Revelation 22:14–15: Those who practice magic are outside of the mercy and grace of God.

Soul Searching (10 minutes)

Have students return to their breakout groups and discuss the items in this section. After allowing time for groups to work, call them back together to report their results. Suggested responses are as follows:

One cannot serve two masters (Matthew 6:24). God demands to have the number one place in our lives. He will not share His throne with another (Matthew 12:25–32).

Often those who are exceptionally meek, shut out of society, or who feel extreme hatred will seek ways to gain secret power over others. However, note that this is not always the case.

If you or someone you know is dabbling in witchcraft, steps must be taken immediately to get help from parents, pastors, or Christian teachers. This is a serious matter.

It takes little to send one down the slippery slope of unbelief. The devil is looking for any opportunity to draw us away from the true God (1 Peter 5:8). Curiosity is one of the devil's tools.

God promises that He will listen to the prayers of all who believe. He also promises to forgive those who turn away from their sins. God desires that all people be saved and come to a knowledge of the truth (1 Timothy 2:8). He continues to nudge His children by the Gospel. He alone can break through the bonds of sin and Satan, turning people to Himself. We need not rely on our own strength; He has done all of the work of salvation.

Closing (2 minutes)

Close with a group prayer. Be sure to include prayers for those who may be lost in the deception of Wicca. Include any specific prayer requests that students may mention.

Resources

- Dave Hunt, *Occult Invasion* (Eugene, Oregon: Harvest House Publishers, 1998)

- Craig S. Hawkins, *Witchcraft—Exploring the World of Wicca* (Grand Rapids, Michigan: Baker Books, 1996)

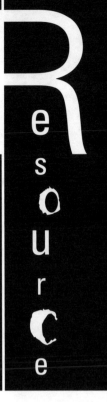

Definition

Simply defined, witchcraft is "the use of sorcery or magic" (*Merriam Webster's Collegiate Dictionary, Tenth Edition*). The term *witch* comes from the Old English word *wicca*. Witchcraft often falls under the category of paganism (the beliefs of one who has no religion) and is closely associated with magick (the forbidden art of attempting to call upon spirit power). Females are frequently called witches and males are called wizards or warlocks. Those within the religion refer to themselves as the Old Religion, Druids (sorcerers), or simply The Craft.

Beliefs

Witches believe that the Ultimate Deity (energy source) is manifested in the male god called LORD and female goddess called LADY. Witches claim to receive their ultimate power through these sources. Their worship services are held in secret. They meet from midnight until dawn on each of the 13 full moons. These meetings are referred to as the esbat. There are also 8 major festivals or sabats. Among these is Samhain (the witches' new year), which is celebrated from October 31–November 11.

A witch coven or "congregation" is usually made of 13 people, often with 6 men and 6 women and a high priest or priestess. Witches believe in reincarnation. They believe that at death they go to Summerland to continue their spiritual education before returning to earth.

History

The history of witchcraft dates back to biblical times with the worship of the gods and goddesses of fertility. Calling on magical powers for healing is found in the legends of Mesopotamia, Egypt, and Canaan. When the children of Israel were about to enter the Promised Land, God gave them strict orders to avoid witchcraft and sorcery. King Saul disobeyed God's Law by seeking counsel from a witch instead of from the true God. He died shortly afterward. Today's witch population is estimated between 100,000–200,000.

Goal

The goal of witchcraft can be summed up in one word: power. Witches believe in power coming from the body and have developed ways to try to increase it, collect it, and use it.

Page

2B

You Respond

The following statements are summaries of some of the teachings of *Wicca*. Read each statement and then answer the following question.

Many participants in Wicca may have been raised in homes with traditional religious upbringing. Their quest for spiritual insight typically began by dabbling with Ouija boards, tarot cards, and other alternative materials.

How can something as seemingly harmless as tarot cards, Ouija boards, psychic hotlines, and so on become a first step on the pathway to the destruction of our soul?

Wiccans feel that the traditional churches are being untruthful with their followers. They do not believe in the existence of heaven and hell.

How can you tell if your church is the true church? What is the only source of real truth? Is there really a hell? How do you know?

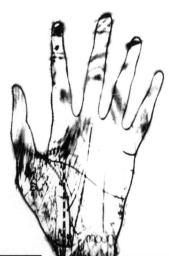

Reincarnation is a central teaching for Wicca.
What does **Hebrews 9:27** say in response?

Wiccans don't believe in heaven or hell, they feel that such teachings are of the "old way," a general term used for traditional Judeo/Christian beliefs.

Why would someone want to believe in a religion that does not include hell or the devil?

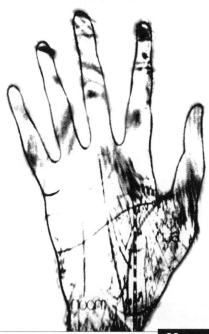

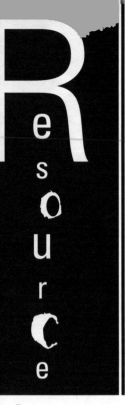

God Speaks

The Bible uses many different terms that would fall under the heading of witchcraft today. Write the term used in each Scripture passage:

Ezekiel 13:23

Exodus 8:19

Isaiah 8:19

Isaiah 47:9

Micah 5:12

God made His view of witchcraft very clear. There is no way one can misunderstand or misinterpret what God means in these Scripture passages: Read **Deuteronomy 18:10–13** and **Revelation 22:14–15**.

Soul-Searching

Those connected with pagan religions will often tell you that they do not require you to give up your current faith. They claim you can believe in both your religion and their religion. How would you answer them? See **Matthew 6:24; 12:25–32.**

Why is achieving special power so important to some people? What type of individual feels the need for more power?

What should you do if you know of a friend who is dabbling in witchcraft?

Why should we not even begin to satisfy a slight curiosity about witchcraft by reading a few books or attending a witches' meeting (coven)?

What does God promise to those who refrain from or turn from these practices **(1 Peter 3:10–12; James 5:19–20)**? Remember, we cannot turn away from sin and back to God whenever we choose. That is one of Satan's lies. God is the one with the power to call and change people's lives. Know that He does it gladly and willingly.

3

Sanctuaries of Darkness—
Voodoo Religions

Lesson Focus

Combining elements of the West African Yoruba tribal beliefs with elements of Roman Catholicism, voodoo is a folk religion that leads its followers away from the true God. It is only through faith in Jesus Christ that we have eternal life.

Objectives

By the power of the Holy Spirit, the participants, through the study of God's Word, will

1. gain an understanding of the danger of combining Christian teachings and pagan ritual as found in voodoo;

2. be strengthened in their faith in the one true God—Jesus Christ, their Savior.

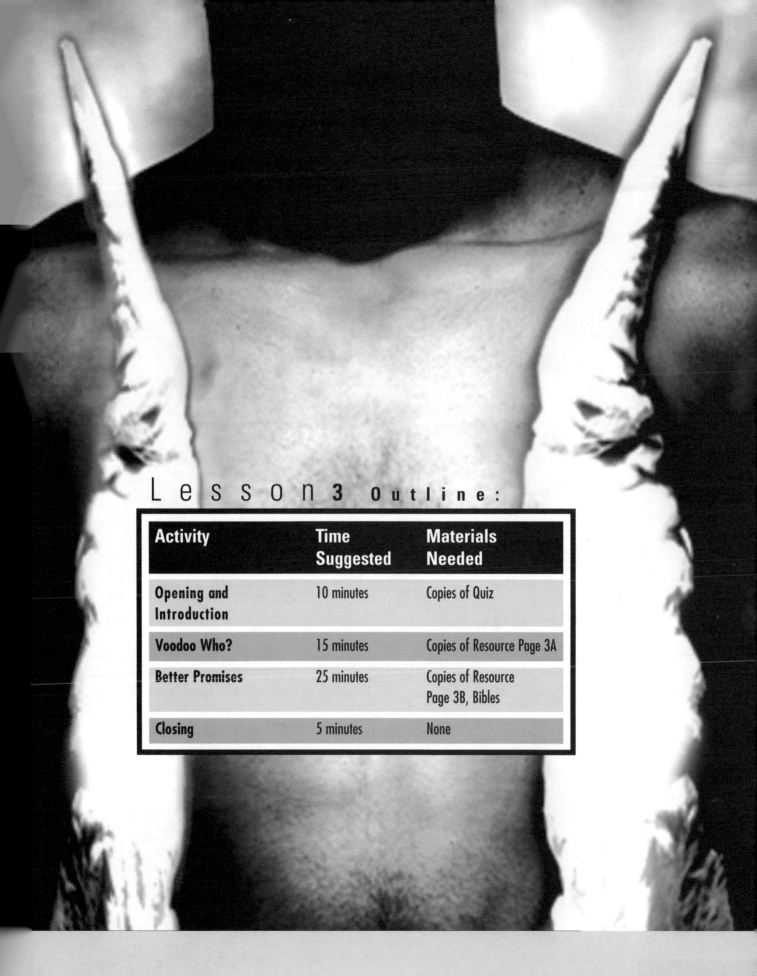

Lesson **3** Outline:

Activity	Time Suggested	Materials Needed
Opening and Introduction	10 minutes	Copies of Quiz
Voodoo Who?	15 minutes	Copies of Resource Page 3A
Better Promises	25 minutes	Copies of Resource Page 3B, Bibles
Closing	5 minutes	None

Opening and Introduction (10 minutes)

Begin with prayer: "Dear Father in heaven, we know that You love and care for us because You gave Your Son for us. Take away all fears and concerns that we have at this moment, so that we can concentrate on Your Word. Give us Your Holy Spirit to strengthen us when we are tempted to depart from Your will, and comfort us with Your forgiveness when we are troubled by our sins. In the name of Jesus, Your Son and our Savior. Amen."

The world of voodoo will be unfamiliar to most participants in the class. Introduce the topic by distributing copies of the matching quiz printed below.

___1. Poteau mitan	a. voodoo drum
___2. Loa	b. spirit, god
___3. Santeria	c. voodoo priestess
___4. Houngan	d. sacred pillar in voodoo temple
___5. Mambo	e. store for Santeria supplies
___6. Voudoun	f. religion of Dahomey in West Africa
___7. Agwe	g. multiple expressions of god, deities
___8. Humfort (humfo)	h. Way of the Saints, Rule of Orisha
___9. Yoruba	i. religious sanctuary
___10. Botanica	j. good soul or angel of a person
___11. Orisha	k. initiate at voodoo initiation
___12. Ti bon ange	l. symbolic pattern on voodoo temple floor
___13. Maman	m. gods of Santeria
___14. Hounsis	n. voodoo god of the sea
___15. Vever	o. voodoo priest

[Answers: 1,d; 2,g; 3,h; 4,o; 5,c; 6,b; 7,n; 8,i; 9,f; 10,e; 11,m; 12,j; 13,a; 14,k; 15,l]

Point out that entering into the world of strange religions or cults is like visiting a country with a totally different language. But the secretive language that cults typically use attracts the curious and exercises power over them.

While attending a National Youth Gathering in New Orleans, two Gathering participants spent some time in a store full of voodoo dolls, beads, rosaries, statues, crucifixes, candles, herbs, shells, oils, bones, and other "supplies." They purchased a couple of items. A third youth who did not have the nerve to enter the store said that what they did was dangerous. Ask the class, "Do you think this person had a valid concern?" Have the class read Ephesians 5:11–13 and ask, "How does what Paul said here apply to situations like this?"

Voodoo Who? (15 minutes)

Distribute copies of Resource Page 3A. Briefly review the four sections on this page: (1) Voodoo Who? (2) The Secrets of Voodoo, (3) Sanctuaries of Santeria (a version of voodoo practiced in the U.S.), and (4) False Spirituality. Allow students time to ask questions for understanding.

Better Promises (25 minutes)

Distribute copies of Resource Page 3B. Interaction with unseen spiritual powers was a major problem among the Christians in Colossae. See Colossians 1:13, 16; 2:8, 10, 15, 18, 20. The letter of Colossians is Paul's response. The bottom line is that Christ is supreme. He has disarmed the powers of darkness (Colossians 1:15–20).

Divide the class into pairs, assigning the statements and asking them to discuss the teachings/practices of voodoo in light of the two questions in the second paragraph. Invite the pairs to share their insights. As you help the participants evaluate voodoo, note the following Scriptural themes in the passages listed:

God the Creator is identified not as some creative force that exists in the creation. He is the Father of our Lord Jesus Christ, "from whom all things came and for whom we live" (1 Corinthians 8:6). Jesus shares with His Father the work of creation and preservation. Yet there is only one God.

The passages here focus on the *transcendence* of God. God is "absolutely free and superior to all earthly, material things; even the heaven and heaven of heavens cannot contain Him" (*Lutheran Cyclopedia,* 774). See 1 Kings 8:27 and Job 11:7–10.

God is not dependent on human sacrifices. Rather, in the name of Jesus, who is our once-and-for-all perfect sacrifice for sin, we bring our requests to God. When we bring our troubles to Him, we also, in the same breath, thank and praise Him for His goodness.

Using a Bible dictionary, help participants understand what is meant by each of the items listed in Deuteronomy 18:9–13. Also consult the explanation of the Second Commandment, which addresses satanic arts (Martin Luther in *Luther's Small Catechism with Explanation* [St. Louis: Concordia Publishing House, 1986], pp. 63–64).

The voodoo religion is based on fear, and attempts are constantly made to keep the unseen deities (*loa*) happy and satisfied. Christians place their trust in the true God who surrounds them with His mighty protection. Because of Christ, God is for us, not against us (Romans 8:31). There is nothing to fear for those whose trust is in Him.

God's cleansing is the forgiveness of sins earned for us through the blood of Christ shed for us on the cross (Colossians 1:13–14; 1 Peter 1:18–19).

Closing (5 minutes)

Religions like voodoo feed on the fears of participants (bad luck, misfortune, sickness, accidents, poverty, and violence) by promising to help them. Ask the group to return to their pairs and to spend three minutes sharing common fears people may have. Encourage each of them to read to their partner the words of promise and assurance in Psalm 91:9–16.

Close with prayer: "God of truth and life, we thank and praise You for delivering us from the powers of darkness and making us members of Your Son's kingdom. Help us to realize that this world is still a place of spiritual danger where forces seek to draw us away from our Savior and the life He gives. Strengthen us with Your Word and daily restore in us the joy of our salvation. In Jesus' name. Amen."

Resources

Dictionary of Cults, Sects, Religions, and the Occult (Grand Rapids, Michigan: Zondervan Publishing, 1993)

www.religioustolerance.org/santeri.htm

Voodoo Who?

Voodoo is a folk religion practiced by growing numbers of people in places like Florida, New York, and Los Angeles. Voodoo was the native religion of the Yoruba tribes in West Africa, originally brought to the Caribbean region (Haiti, Cuba) in the 1800s through the slave trade. Voodoo is a mixture of the Yoruba tribal religion and certain Roman Catholic beliefs.

The Secrets of Voodoo

Voodoo devotees believe in a creator (*Voudoun,* "universal energy") and in numerous other gods or spiritual entities called *loa* or *orisha*. These gods are believed to be the spirits of dead people (such as saints, ancestors, or prominent persons) who interact with the living. Through various ceremonies these spirits can temporarily possess a voodoo worshiper and influence the person's life for either good or evil.

Sanctuaries of Santeria

Santeria (Spanish, "worship of saints") is one form of voodoo. Santerians usually have these beliefs and practices:

Beliefs

Deities: Olurun is the supreme god. Orisha are lesser "guardians" who need food through animal sacrifices and meals. They especially need praise.

Sacrifices: In rituals, an animal's blood (usually a chicken's) is offered to Orisha to please saints, bring good luck, and forgive sins.

Possession: Rhythms and dances bring possession by an Orisha. This is desired by voodoo participants as part of a spiritual high that may result in supernatural good.

Ancestor worship: Ancestors bring moral guidance.

Practices

Secrecy: Beliefs are secret and shared only with those who are initiated into the practice.

Tradition: Beliefs are not transmitted by books, but by individual teachers.

Ritual: The invocation of Olurun and the rhythm produced by drums, dancing, and sacrifices are examples of ritual.

Priesthood: Priests and priestesses have various powers, including healing.

Botanicas: Stores with Santerian supplies such as charms, herbs, potions, and musical instruments are called botanicas.

False Spirituality

Voodoo looks harmless, but it belongs to the kingdom of darkness and opposes God's truth revealed in Jesus Christ, our Savior. God's Word cautions, "See to it that no one takes you captive through hollow and deceptive philosophy, which depends on human tradition and the basic principles of this world rather than on Christ" (**Colossians 2:8**).

Page

3A

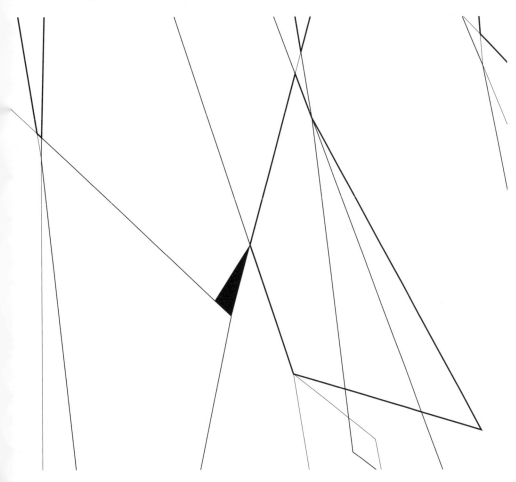

Better Promises

In Christ "are hidden all the treasures of wisdom and knowledge" (**Colossians 2:3**). "Christ is all and is in all" (**Colossians 3:11**). Those who believe in Him have all the blessings He won for them through His death on the cross and victorious resurrection (**Colossians 2:13–15**).

Voodoo religions are preoccupied with fortune, health, and success. Good luck and protection from evil happenings are foremost concerns. Listed below are six ways voodooists seek security and meaning in life. As you study God's Word together, share (1) how voodooism fails to measure up to God's will, and especially (2) how Christianity has much more to offer than voodooism because it is built on "better promises" (**Hebrews 8:6**).

Polytheism is the worship of many gods. Voodoo believes in many divine entities. See **1 Corinthians 8:4–6**; **Deuteronomy 6:4**; and **Isaiah 42:8**.

Animism is the belief that spirit beings (often ancestors) inhabit objects such as trees and stones.

Voodoo is animistic, deriving from tribal religions that believe a *soul* or *life force* exists in or attaches to created things (like trees and animals). See **Genesis 1:1**; **Colossians 1:15–17**; and **Psalm 104:24–25**.

Sacrifices with the blood of animals in voodoo are thought to bring physical and spiritual benefits to the sacrificer or to the one for whom the sacrifice is being made. Sacrifices also serve as food for the spirit entities. See **Psalm 50:15,** paying careful attention to the context established in verses **7–14**. Also see **Hebrews 9:12–14; 10:4, 12**.

Occultic practices such as sorcery, magic, seances, and divination are common in voodoo. Santerian priests and priestesses use shells to foretell the future. See **Deuteronomy 18:9–13; Leviticus 19:31**; and **Colossians 3:1–4**.

Good luck and divine *protection* come when you are on the good side of the voodoo spirits and/or saints. See **Psalm 34:7; Luke 21:18**; and **Romans 8:28, 37–39**.

Cleansing and *healing* are expected through rituals of voodoo priests. See **1 John 1:7–9** and **Psalm 51:7–12**.

Page

3B

4

Satanism—
The Ultimate Abomination

Lesson Focus

There are two equal and opposite errors into which our race can fall about the devils. One is to disbelieve in their existence. The other is to believe and to feel an unhealthy interest in them. [Satan] is equally pleased by both errors. —C.S. Lewis, *The Screwtape Letters*.

Objectives

By the power of the Holy Spirit, the participants, through the study of God's Word, will

1. gain an understanding of Satan's true motives and the results of his work;

2. understand that by His death and resurrection Christ has totally defeated Satan and his power over us.

Lesson 4 Outline:

Activity	Time Suggested	Materials Needed
Opening	5 minutes	None
The Scary Facts	10 minutes	Copies of Resource Page 4A
Power Play	15 minutes	Copies of Resource Page 4B, Bibles
Soul Searching Questions	20 minutes	Copies of Resource Page 4B, Bibles
Closing	5 minutes	None

Opening (5 minutes)

To open you may wish to discuss the quote from C. S. Lewis's *The Screwtape Letters* found on this page. Ask students to tell how they see this statement to be true. With a word of prayer, ask God to bless your study and time together.

The Scary Facts (10 minutes)

Distribute copies of Resource Page 4A. Allow students to review information and discuss together.

Be careful not to give students the impression that our daily sins make us satanists. To be a satanist one must willingly despise the true God and give allegiance to Satan. Those within the formal Satan-worshiping community need our prayers, especially when you consider that most dabbling satanists tend to be teenagers. Discuss with the group what the profile of someone who is involved in satanism would be.

Satanism dates back many years. However, students tend to be more interested in more recent developments. Much information about satanism is available on the Internet. One site includes a three-page, single-spaced letter entitled "A Letter to Satanic Youth" that heralds the following of Satan and openly despises parents, God, and the establishment.

It is interesting that Anton LaVey, the author of *The Satanic Bible*, claimed that he wished not so much to actually worship Satan (at times he even denied Satan's existence) as to go contrary to established morals, society, and traditional religions. LaVey's church received a revival at the first release of the movie *Rosemary's Baby*, in which LaVey played the role of Satan.

Power Play (15 minutes)

Distribute copies of Resource Page 4B to each student. Allow students to work together in breakout groups to list examples of each of the kinds of power described. Call the groups together and record their findings on four master lists. Discuss the students' findings.

Ask students to return to their groups and complete the remainder of this section. As time allows, discuss the answers that students find in Scripture.

Satan speaks only in lies (John 8:44). Remember, anything that is partly, but not completely true is also a lie.

Satan's work has been destroyed by Christ (1 John

3:8) even though it may not always be obvious. One of Satan's deceptions is the impression that he has power equal to God's.

Satan tempted Jesus to worship him. Jesus refused and said, "Worship the Lord your God and fear Him only" (Matthew 4:10). Satan clearly has no power over Christ and God's Word (Matthew 4:8–10).

Allegiance to Satan ensnares, even if it isn't obvious at first. True freedom is found only in Christ.

Soul Searching Questions (20 minutes)

Have students work together in groups or individually to complete the questions from this section. Allow time for discussion of their answers. Be sure to get to the answers that remind us of Christ's victory over sin and Satan. Suggested responses include the following:

Desensitizers have lured many unsuspecting young Christians away from God and into Satan's web.

Satan can give power. However, since Christ has defeated Satan, Satan's power is limited to whatever God allows.

While drawing a pentagram does not mean someone is a follower of Satan, it may provide a great opportunity to ask your friend if she knows what the symbol means and find out how she feels about it.

Satan does exist! To trifle with him or to deceive ourselves into thinking that he is weak or powerless can be a devastating and even fatal error (1 Peter 5:8).

God supplies us with sufficient armor to fight off Satan (Ephesians 6:10–18).

Satan has been defeated and will be put away forever on the Last Day. We have God's Word (Romans 16:20).

The Holy Spirit and Christ within you are greater than the power of Satan (1 John 4:4).

The words of this great Reformation hymn remind us of God's victory over sin and the devil—a single word of God can defeat Satan.

Closing (5 minutes)

Close with a group prayer. Ask God to give you strength to resist the devil's temptations. Thank God for defeating Satan so that we now have the promise of eternal life. Be sure to include any specific prayer requests that students may have.

Resources

🕮 Roland Cap Ehlke, *Christianity, Cults, and World Religions* (Milwaukee, Wisconsin: Northwestern Publishing House, 1993)

👁 Rick Lawrence, *Evil and the Occult* (Loveland, Colorado: Group Publishing, 1994)

🕮 Bruce G. Frederickson, *How to Respond to Satanism* (St. Louis: Concordia Publishing House, 1995)

👁 Bob Larson, *Satanism—The Seduction of America's Youth* (Nashville, Tennessee: Thomas Nelson, 1989)

🕮 Siegbert W. Becker, *Wizards that Peep* (Milwaukee, Wisconsin: Northwestern Publishing House, 1978)

🕷 **www.satanism101.com**

🕷 **www.satanicchurch.com**

👁 **www.religioustolerance.org**

Extending the Lesson

Anton LaVey's The Satanic Bible contains nine statements that clarify his doctrines. Read the summaries of each statement aloud and discuss with students how the statements compare to the Beatitudes as found in Matthew 5: 3–12.

Satan represents indulgence instead of abstinence.

Satan represents vital existence instead of spiritual pipe dreams.

Satan represents undefiled wisdom instead of hypocritical self-deceit.

Satan represents kindness to those who deserve it instead of love wasted on ingrates.

Satan represents vengeance instead of turning the other cheek.

Satan represents responsibility to the responsible instead of concern for psychic vampires.

Satan represents man as just another animal, sometimes better but more often worse than those who walk on all fours; because of his divine spiritual and intellectual development, man has become the most vicious animal of all.

Satan represents all of the so-called sins, as they all lead to physical, mental, or emotional gratification.

Satan has been the best friend the church has ever had, as he has kept it in business all these years.

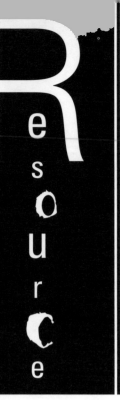

The Scary Facts

Definition

Sin is disobedience against God. Satan wants to keep people separate from God and His forgiving love. It is true that by sinning one follows the desires of Satan, yet the religion of satanism is more than that. It includes obedience, worship, and even openly praying to Satan. The satanist gives his life to the evil schemes of Satan and revels in being possessed by the Prince of Darkness.

Satanists are generally divided into two groups:

Formal Worshipers—These are official members of the Church of Satan. They follow the teachings of *The Satanic Bible* and participate in satanic worship services. The Church of Satan has recently made special efforts to invite teens into their organization.

Dabbling Satanists—This group is far more prevalent among teenagers. Many of Satan's followers are young people rebelling against their families, church, or culture. As they seek attention, they like shocking those around them by making others think they are befriending the devil himself. This is the group most likely to be mentioned in newspaper articles about cemetery vandalism, satanic graffiti, and an occasional animal sacrifice.

History

Recent developments in Satanism can be traced back to Aliester Crowley (1875–1947), who claimed to be the "wickedest man in the world." Crowley's writings are very popular in the satanic movement today.

Anton LaVey (died October 29, 1997, although his death certificate lists October 31—Halloween) was the author of *The Satanic Bible* and organized the Church of Satan in 1966. He shocked America with the satanic baptism of his three-year-old daughter, Karla. As an adult, Karla followed in her late father's footsteps by reorganizing his church on October 31, 1999 into the First Church of Satan. There are also other loosely established satanic churches. The Church of Satan is still the largest organized satanic church with self-claimed membership estimated in the thousands.

2001 Concordia Publishing House, St Louis. Reproduced by permission. Scripture: NIV®.

Satanic Symbols

Have you seen any of these signs? Discuss how they are used.

THE PENTAGRAM

The pentagram is the five-pointed star. One point represents the spirit. The other points represent wind, fire, earth, and water. It is believed to have power to conjure good spirits and ward off evil spirits.

THE SIGIL OF BAPHOMET

This figure uses an inverted pentagram that includes the figure of a goat, with the points representing the goat's two horns, two ears, and goatee (see **Matthew 25:32–33**). It is the registered trademark of the Church of Satan.

THE NUMBERS 666 (or sometimes the letters FFF)

This symbol relates directly to the mark of the beast as found in **Revelation 13:18**.

THE HORNED HAND

This is a sign of recognition to others within the occult.

THE INVERTED CROSS

Many of the rituals of satanism attempt to do the inverse of Christianity: for example, using the word NEMA in place of AMEN, reading the Lord's Prayer in reverse, or covering the altar with a black cloth. In a similar way the inverted cross is a mockery of Christianity and what it stands for.

Power Play

We can see forms of power displayed on many levels. Give several examples of people or things that use power in the following ways:

MENTAL POWER:

PHYSICAL POWER:

EMOTIONAL POWER:

SPIRITUAL POWER:

Many satanic followers are obsessed with gaining power over those around them. Through obtaining special satanic knowledge, they feel they are above others, thus gaining a status of superiority. Satanism promises freedom from bondage to parents, society, and especially God.

When Satan promises power, he neglects to mention a few key points.

What is Satan's native language (**John 8:44**)?

What is the condition of Satan's work (**1 John 3:8**)?

What happened the only time Satan worship is mentioned in Scripture (**Matthew 4:8–10**)?

How would you respond to this statement? "Satanists believe God enslaves His people, but Satan truly gives his people freedom." For help, use the following passages:
**2 Timothy 2:26; Proverbs 5:22;
2 Corinthians 3:17; Romans 8:18–21;
John 8:31–32, 36; and Galatians 5:1–2.**

Soul Searching Questions

How are desensitizers, such as astrology, tarot cards, Ouija boards, or role-playing games like Dungeons and Dragons, frequently used by Satan? Where do you see signs of satanism in the music world?

Satan promises power. Can he really give people special power, and if so, how much (see **Job 1:12; 2:6**)?

Have you seen open or subtle signs of satanism? Where? How would you respond to a friend whom you just saw draw a pentagram on her notebook cover?

Why should Christians take satanism seriously (**1 Peter 5:8**)?

How can we find comfort from the message of **Ephesians 6:10–18**? In **Romans 16:20**? In **1 John 4:4**?

Read the words of Martin Luther's "**A Mighty Fortress**" (*Lutheran Worship* 297 and 298; *All God's People Sing* 90). How does Luther treat the problem of Satan in the world?

5

Sprinkling of the Sacred—
Mysticism and Multiple Spiritual Beliefs

Lesson Focus

Studies tell us that today's youth are deeply spiritual. Upon closer examination, however, we see that this spirituality involves a smorgasbord of Christian beliefs and non-Christian traditions. Salvation can be found only through faith in Jesus Christ, who lived, died, and lives to conquer Satan.

Objectives

By the power of the Holy Spirit, the participants, through the study of God's Word, will

1. see how combining Christianity with other religious traditions and rituals can lead to false belief;

2. focus on the true Spirit of God who brings us to saving faith in Jesus Christ.

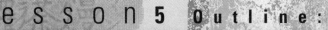

Lesson 5 Outline:

Activity	Time Suggested	Materials Needed
Opening and Introduction	10 minutes	Newsprint and markers
Sprinkling of the Sacred	15 minutes	Copies of Resource Page 5A
Search for Spirituality	20 minutes	Copies of Resource Page 5B
Closing	10 minutes	Bibles

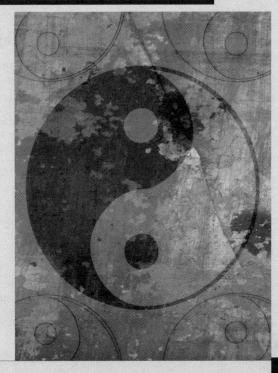

Opening and Introduction (10 minutes)

Open with prayer: "Heavenly Father, Your Word is a lamp to our feet and a light for our path. In Your Word, You revealed the mystery of Your love for us in Jesus, Your Son. You have also promised the gift of Your Holy Spirit to bring us inner peace. Forgive us for searching elsewhere for meaning and purpose in life. Help us discover the joys of following You. Give us Your wisdom and guidance now as we seek a deeper understanding of Your grace and will for our lives. In Jesus' name. Amen."

The July 2000 issue of *Seventeen* magazine reports on a poll of 13,000 readers. Most (82 percent) consider themselves religious. But 48 percent chose to create religion on their own terms: "These teens pick and choose the principles they uphold, which sometimes means they don't attend a traditional worship."

Tom Beaudoin (*Virtual Faith: The Irreverent Spiritual Quest of Generation X)* writes, "There's a real thirst for community, joy and relationships that drives young people into thinking about spiritual life."

Post a sheet of newsprint with the following heading: "To respond to the needs of kids today, I wish my church would ..." Give the class participants seven to eight minutes to give their responses. Introduce the topic of the lesson by saying something such as, "Our society offers all kinds of opportunities for young people to satisfy their search for spirituality. Let's look at this issue, keeping in mind that God has called us to be His instruments in carrying out His plan to bring spiritual life and fulfillment to the world in Jesus Christ."

Sprinkling of the Sacred (15 minutes)

A popular magazine introduces a "soul poll" by asking its readers to explore their spirituality. From Aretha Franklin, who belts out tunes like "Spirit in the Dark," to Madonna, who on her album *Ray of Light* sings about *shanti* (the Sanskrit word for inner peace), celebrities everywhere seem to be publicizing their spiritual yearnings. Spirituality has now become a popular buzzword, and it covers beliefs and practices ranging from martial arts' *zazen* (meditation originating in Buddhism) to Native American *talking circles* (passing a rock to someone who then gives a spiritual reflection).

What spiritual yearnings do people have today? Why don't they seek to satisfy them in churches? What is different about today's secular search for spirituality in comparison to the way Christians receive and practice their spiritual life? You may want to ask whether the participants agree with the following statement from *Psychology Today* in an article entitled "Spirituality": "Behind the quest for spirituality lies a growing need for passion and depth in our lives."

Distribute copies of Resource Page 5A. The title "Sprinkling of the Sacred" is intended to signal an underlying theme of this lesson: today people understand religion in very broad terms, drawing spiritual elements from many sources. A common feature of most modern spiritualities is the exploration of the inner-self (often regarded as divine) to discover divine truth and guidance.

Briefly review the four topics on the first resource page: (1) Experiencing God..., (2) Becoming One with "God," (3) A Sprinkling of the Sacred, and (4) The Mystery of Christ.

The goal of this page is for participants to realize and appreciate that God has promised to reveal Himself to human beings only through the Scriptures and to give His spiritual blessings only through the means of grace (Word and Sacraments). We cannot know a gracious God except through the revelation of the "mystery of Christ," the Gospel (Ephesians 3:1–6).

Search for Spirituality (20 minutes)

The five statements on Resource Page 5B are written to help the participants examine some of the basic themes of current spirituality in a positive way. The overall aim is to help the participants understand the search for spirituality as an opportunity to bring the richness of God's grace in Christ to others (Romans 9:23; 11:33; Ephesians 1:7, 18; 2:7; 3:8, 16; Colossians 1:27; 2:2). The five quotations suggest the following points for discussion:

The first statement is based on the following New Age principles:

All is one; therefore all is God.

Mankind is divine and has unlimited potential.

Mankind's basic flaw is ignorance of his divinity.

Mankind's basic need is personal transformation produced by consciousness-altering techniques.

(From Eldon Winker, *The New Age Is Lying to You* [St. Louis: Concordia Publishing House, 1994], 17–23)

The two passages from Romans teach that (1) the human psyche is sinful and (2) the true "life force" is the Spirit of Christ, who died and was raised again to life.

In response to the second statement, assure participants that true transformation and enlightenment come from above, through Jesus Christ who is the light of the world and through His Holy Spirit who works through the Word. St. Paul, therefore, writes in Colossians 3:1–4, "Since, then, you have been raised with Christ, set your hearts on things above, where Christ is seated at the right hand of God. Set your minds on things above, not on earthly things. For you died, and your life is now hidden with Christ in God. When Christ, who is your life, appears, then you also will appear with Him in glory."

Yoga in Hinduism refers to "practices designated to unite the individual mind with ultimate reality." Many people today practice yoga without adopting a Hindu perspective or even being aware of its connection. However, in some cases yoga instructors introduce people to Hindu teachings. Perhaps for most, yoga *(hatha yoga)* is merely a physical exercise. How would we know if a yoga instructor is entering into spirituality?

The quote from Neale Walsch, a popular New Age writer, offers an opportunity to make three important points: (1) God is transcendent, that is, completely above and apart from human beings. He is our Creator, not some divine force within us enabling us to achieve godness. (2) We know God and He speaks to us only by revelation in His Word, not through human experience. (3) If we begin to trust our feelings, we will only become more uncertain and eventually will end in despair. The Holy Spirit leads us to trust God's Word and builds our faith on what is true and certain.

She Said Yes is the story of Cassie Bernall, one of the students gunned down at Columbine High School. In this book Cassie's mother says, "That is why I am able, ultimately, to see the loss of my daughter not so much as a defeat, but as a victory. The pain is no less. It will always remain deep and raw. Even so, I know that her death was not a waste, but a triumph of honesty and courage. To me, Cassie's life says that it is better to die for what you believe than to live a lie." Read Romans 8:31–39. Point out that the only true victory lies not in our honesty or courage, or in any other belief, but in Christ Jesus who has defeated our enemies and keeps us secure in His everlasting love.

Closing (10 minutes)

Prayer and meditation are a part of a Christian's daily life. Divide your group in pairs. Ask them to meditate for one minute on Romans 8:37–39 and discuss what it means personally to them.

Close in prayer: "Lord Jesus, we cannot thank You enough for the way Your love has personally touched our lives. You have made us Your children through Baptism and have surrounded us with Your protection and care. In times when we especially need Your comfort and support, draw us to Your strong Word for strength and inner peace. In Your name we pray. Amen."

Sprinkling of the Sacred

Mysticism and Multiple Spiritual Beliefs

Experiencing God...

Mysticism usually refers to "claims of immediate knowledge of Ultimate Reality (whether or not this is called 'God') by direct personal experience" (*The Oxford Dictionary of the Christian Church* [1997], 1127). Simplified, it refers to a fascination with and attraction to the mysterious and unexplainable. Often mysticism may be so taken by the mysterious that it ignores the obvious. Historically, mysticism or mystical tendencies have been present in most religions, including Christianity.

Becoming One with "God"

The goal of mysticism is to attain "union with god," to achieve a state of "absorption of the soul into the divine" directly through such practices as meditation, contemplation, prayer, and other spiritual activities. Mystics often cite religious experiences and feelings of peace and happiness as proof that they have had an encounter with the divine. They also point to such phenomena as dreams, trances, visions, and spiritual highs.

A Sprinkling of the Sacred

Mysticism can be found in non-Christian religions such as Hinduism (*yoga*), Buddhism (*zazen*), Judaism (*kabbalah*, in its modern form *Hasidism*), and Islam (*Sufism*). Christian mystics sometimes speak of four steps or stages needed to ascend to a mystical state of union with God: the purgative way (purification of the soul), the illuminative way (feeling of enlightenment and love of God), the unitive way (consciousness of God's presence in the soul), and spiritual marriage (ecstatic state of perfect union).

Sprinkled throughout New Age thought and practices today are techniques for "God-realization." New Agers talk about getting in touch with "the divine soul within" themselves (the New Age movement teaches that humankind is individually and collectively god, and that a person can create his or her own reality and truth). New Age mysticism involves such things as transcendental meditation, channeling, spirit guides, conversations with god, clairvoyance, reincarnation, and various other methods of reaching "the realization of godself."

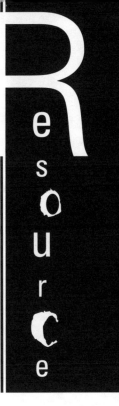

The Mystery of Christ

Christians can rejoice that God has made known "the mystery of Christ," the Gospel, through the Scriptures. The Gospel is the "unveiled secret" of His love revealed in the fullness of time in Jesus Christ our Savior (**Ephesians 3:2–6**). Only through this Gospel and the sacraments of Baptism and Holy Communion do we become one with God and enjoy His blessings of peace and joy!

Search for Spirituality

People today are on a new quest for spirituality. We Christians can see this positively. This search opens up many opportunities to share the real source of our spiritual fulfillment, joy, and peace—Jesus Christ! While many religious movements are peppered with what appears to be sacred or holy, in reality these movements draw people away from the truth in Christ, our Savior. Below are some examples of the new spirituality present today. Use the following statements (share other examples too) and the Bible passages as discussion points. Focus on the great news that Christians can share with others!

"Contemplation, meditation, prayer, rituals and other spiritual practices have the power to release the 'life force' in the deepest levels of the human psyche" (*Psychology Today,* Sept./Oct. 1999, 45). **Romans 7:18; 8:5–11**

Music celebrity Madonna has said that a form of Jewish mysticism called *kabbalah* has transformed her life. Kabbalah makes use of numerology, astrology, teaching about reincarnation and karma, and the pursuit of enlightenment through "scanning" of a mystical text called the *Zohar.* **John 1:9–13 and Ephesians 1:17–18**

Referring to the practice of yoga, *Glamour* magazine asks, "Do you find peace of mind in the pillows—or in the pews?" **Philippians 4:4–7; Psalm 122; and Ephesians 5:15–20**

In the best seller *Conversations with God, Book I*, New Age writer Neale Walsch carries on conversations with his "divine self" [god]. Walsch wrote that god told him this: "Simply *live* [what god says]. *Experience* [what god says]. Then live whatever other paradigm you want to construct. Afterward, look to your *experience* to find your truth" (p. 109). **John 14:5–6; 6:32–35**

Cassie Bernall dabbled in various spiritual activities, including at one point such things as death rock, vampires, and self-mutilation. At a youth retreat she came to know Jesus Christ and the good news of His forgiveness. Before she died in the Columbine High School shootings, her killer asked her, "Do you believe in God?" She then spoke the last word of her life, "Yes." Cassie's mother ended her book *She Said Yes* with these words, "To me, Cassie's life says that it is better to die for what you believe, than to live a lie." **Romans 6:1–10; 8:37–39** (What do you think of this statement by Cassie's mom?)

Page

5B

Creatures of the Night— Vampires and Werewolves

Lesson Focus

Students often look for ways to gain control in their lives when they feel they have lost all control. Fantasy worlds, horror films, and role-playing games often introduce dark realms where an adept player who invests lots of time may gain some form of control. In reality this false feeling of control may leave the user under the control of the dark realm. God's plan for our life is to live in His light, away from all darkness. In Him is the light of life, a new life in Jesus Christ.

Objectives

By the power of the Holy Spirit, the participants, through the study of God's Word, will

1. recognize the desire we have for control in our lives;

2. reject the darkness found in fantasy worlds;

3. encourage others to reject the lure of darkness;

4. celebrate the light of life found in Jesus Christ.

Lesson 6 Outline:

Activity	Time Suggested	Materials Needed
Prayer	5 minutes	None
What Would You Do?	5 minutes	3 Scenarios from page 64
The History and Background	10 minutes	Copies of Resource page 6A
Light vs. Darkness	10 minutes	Bibles, newsprint, markers, copies of Resource Page 6B
What Do We Do Now?	15 minutes	Copies of Resource Page 6B, Bibles
Final Things to Remember	10 minutes	None
Closing Prayer	5 minutes	None

Prayer (5 minutes)

Open the session with a prayer: "Heavenly Father, You are the light of the world. We marvel at Your splendor and brightness. By Your light that shines from Your cross, cleanse our lives. Expose the darkness in this world. Shine Your light through us to others. In Jesus' name we pray. Amen."

What Would You Do? (5 minutes)

Introduce this topic by reading the following scenarios and getting responses from the students. These may or may not seem like a big deal to the students, but they are all linked to occultic activity.

Scenario 1

A group of students from school dress completely in black and hang out together at lunch. They invite you to go out with them on Friday night. You have heard that they like to hang out at cemeteries because it's scary. What might you do? Why?

Scenario 2

Your friend just bought a new game that he wants to play. It's called "Vampire: The Masquerade." You've heard it involves incantations, spells, sorcery, and a preoccupation with the dead, but supposedly its very intense and fun. He invites you over to play this weekend. What do you do? Why?

Scenario 3

The new movie *Night of the Werewolf* comes to the theater nearby and your friend's mother is going to buy you and your friend tickets. The movie is rated R for blood and violence. You also know it mocks Christianity and introduces anti-Christian sentiments. What do you do? Why?

Encourage the students to respond to each of these scenarios. Explore further if students have their own stories or real-life scenarios with these issues. Wrap up this section by saying something such as, "All of these scenarios are introductions to a world of darkness. Today we are going to contrast this world of darkness with the light of Christ. Let's take a look at an overview of today's topic."

Optional Opening

As a part of the opening or introduction, ask the students to think of as many "lights" as they can (traffic lights, Lite-

Brite, neon lights, Crystal Light, etc.). Write them on a board or newsprint to post for the study.

The History and Background (10 minutes)

Pass out copies of Resource Page 6A on vampires and werewolves. Read through the sheets as a group. Afterward, ask the students if they have other examples of vampires or werewolves that they have seen or heard about.

Light vs. Darkness (10 minutes)

Pass out the copies of Resource Page 6B and tell the students that John often talked about the contrast between light and darkness. Also pass out the large paper and markers to the students. Divide the group into at least two smaller groups. Assign each group verses from John listed below and on the student pages. The assignment for each group is to illustrate or write what is said about light in the passages.

John 1:4 (Christ's life is the light of men.)

John 1:5 (Christ's light shines in the darkness.)

John 1:9 (The true light gives light to every man.)

John 3:19 (People love darkness instead of light.)

John 3:20 (Evildoers hate light.)

John 8:12 (Jesus said He is the light.)

John 9:5 (Again Jesus calls Himself the light.)

1 John 1:5 (There is no darkness in the light.)

Have each group share their findings with the other groups. Ask, "Why do you think Jesus is described as the light?" (Possible answers are—He is all good, there is no sin in Him, or He lights the way for us. In Genesis 1 and Revelation there is divine light that is not produced from any light source.) "Why is there darkness apart from Christ?" (There is no hope. There is sin. Evil hates light.) "How are vampires and werewolves linked to darkness?" (They have no Christ, no light. There is evil in them. They take away from God's light.)

What Do We Do Now? (15 minutes)

Scripture makes it clear that there is a separation of light from darkness. Tell the students, "We have looked at what it means to have the light, but now we are going to see the impact of Christ's light in our lives." Encourage the students to look at the two passages under "What Do We Do Now?" You might divide them up into two different groups and have them report back to the group as a whole.

Acts 19:18–19

At this time many people were coming to faith in Christ, but there was still darkness and evil all around. The new believers struggled to put off darkness. People needed to learn what was evil and why, especially when it seemed rather innocent or was so acceptable in society.

What is cited in this passage as an evil deed? (Sorcery)

How should we treat similar things as Christians? (Have nothing to do with them)

What are some things that believers should avoid as they live in the light of Christ? (Drugs, sex, alcohol, involvement with vampire/werewolf imagery, etc.)

What needs to be "burned" (eliminated) in your life? How does Christ make this happen?

2 Corinthians 6:14–7:1

This is a strong message from Paul about the Christian's relationship with things contrary to God.

What does it mean to be "yoked together"? (To be tied together like oxen)

Why is it impossible to try to have darkness and light at the same time? (Push this one with the students to make them think.)

What does it mean to be a temple for God? (His Spirit lives in us, He created us, and we should avoid all evil.)

How do thoughts of vampires and werewolves contaminate our minds? (They draw our focus away from God.)

Extending the Lesson

Go back to the three scenarios from the beginning. Allow the students to give a new response to each based on the scriptural information they now have.

Final Things to Remember (10 minutes)

Vampires and werewolves are creatures of imagination and darkness. They try to put out the light of Christ and trap us in the darkness of fear. Invite all the students to look up 3 John 1:11. Read it together aloud. We are not to be imitators of evil, but imitators of what is good. We can focus on the light, not the darkness, by the power of the Holy Spirit.

(Do not be <u>imitators</u> of <u>evil</u>.)

Finally, have them read Revelation 22:5. This is a picture of eternity in heaven. The battle over darkness has been won. Stress to the students that God gives the Church His light for salvation.

(There will be no more <u>night</u>. God will give us <u>light</u>.)

Closing Prayer (5 minutes)

Close with a prayer: "Heavenly Father, You have given us the light of the world in Your Son, Jesus Christ. Forgive us for the darkness in our lives and for not always looking to You for strength. Thank You for giving us Your Spirit to dwell in us. Through that same Spirit help us to overcome the darkness of this world and be a light showing Your love. In the name of Jesus we pray. Amen."

RESOURCES

- Rein-Hagen, "Vampire: The Masquerade" (Clarkston, Georgia: White Wolf, 1992)

- Jason Barker, "Youth and the Occult" from *The Watchman Expositor* (vol. 15, no. 6, 1998). Also available online at **www.watchman.org/occult/teenwitch.htm**

- Craig Branch, "Games: Fantasy or Reality?" from *The Watchman Expositor* (vol. 15, no. 6, 1998). Also available online at **www.watchman.org/occult/frpgames2.htm**

- David S. Hart, "Face to Face with Goths" from *Focus on the Family* Web site. **www.family.org/cforum/teachersmag/features/a0008356.html**

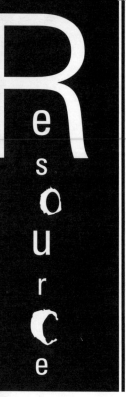

Page

6A

Vampire / Werewolf Fact Sheet

Vampire and werewolf legends were first reported in the twelfth century in Europe. The legendary Count Dracula is a real historical figure—Vlad Tepes, or Vlad the Impaler, a ruthless warrior/ruler who lived in Romania and Transylvania from 1431–1476. A scare about disease and blood swept through Eastern Europe in the late 1600s and early 1700s. Since the days of silent films, movies have popularized these mythical horror figures into our everyday lives.

Some scientists have linked vampire legends to anemia or to a hereditary blood disorder called porphyria, in which the sufferers develop an extreme sensitivity to light, nonhealing sores, excessive hair growth, and a tightening of the skin on the lips and gums, making the teeth very prominent. Werewolf legends may be linked to a genetic disorder called lycanthropy (from the Greek for *wolf* and *man*) in which the sufferer has excessive hair growth covering his entire body.

Many young people are being introduced to a growing subculture that feeds on darkness and fear. The "Goth" movement started in London in 1981 with pale-faced, black-swathed, hair-sprayed night dwellers listening to bands such as The Cure and Depeche Mode. The movie *The Crow* presents stereotypical Goth imagery. Vampirism is an extension of this phenomenon in which followers might go out to cemeteries at night, drink blood, and explore the dark side of life. Some vampire followers go so far as to sleep in coffins, have dental implant fangs, and come out only under the cover of night. Most claim to have psychic abilities.

For those wondering if they might be a vampire, here are some of the characteristics. Vampires are described as misunderstood, demanding attention, night people, easily sunburned, unpredictable, needy, and manipulative. They have a talent for attracting the attention of everyone present. Fortunately, since many people have these characteristics, you have nothing to worry about.

Role-playing games, such as "Vampire: The Masquerade," encourage players to gain insight into a darker half within them, telling stories of madness, lust, and vampires and werewolves that draw players into accounts of the dark side. "The horror of Vampire is the legacy of being a half beast, trapped in a world of no absolutes, where morality is chosen, not ordained" (Rein-Hagen). Those words come from the "Vampire: The Masquerade" player handbook in which players are encouraged to live the game.

In November 1996 a vampire cult lead by a Kentucky teenager named Rod Ferrell murdered two people. The group killed the parents of a young girl who wanted to join the group. The group was captured by authorities on their way to New Orleans. There they planned to meet up with Anne Rice, author of vampire stories such as the popular novel *Interview with a Vampire*.

Buffy the Vampire Slayer is a popular occult-based television show drawing over three million household viewers. Buffy is an average teen who happens to be the "chosen one" to battle vampires, werewolves, and other supernatural beings. Common acceptance of this controversial—though mythical—theme may desensitize Christians to darkness and evil. More and more television shows (even cartoons) are based on occult premises and are introducing students to a dark world of demonic creatures and casting spells.

Resource

Page

6A

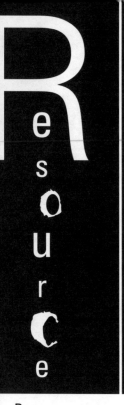
Student Page

Vampires and werewolves are make-believe creatures of darkness. They are portrayed in games, movies, and on television. The darkness of these creatures is in conflict with the light of Christ in our lives. Let's look at what Scripture says about light and darkness.

John 1:4

John 1:5

John 1:9

John 3:19

John 3:20

John 8:12

John 9:5

1 John 1:5

What Do We Do Now?

Acts 19:18–19

At this time many people were coming to faith in Christ, but there was still darkness and evil all around. The new believers struggled to put off darkness.

What is cited in this passage as an evil deed?

How should we treat similar things as Christians?

What are some things believers should avoid as they live in the light of Christ?

What needs to be "burned" in your life? How does Christ make this happen?

2 Corinthians 6:14–7:1

This is a strong message from Paul about the

Christian's relationship with things contrary to God.

What does it mean to be "yoked together"?

Why is it impossible to try to have darkness and light at the same time?

What does it mean to be a temple for God?

How do thoughts of vampires and werewolves contaminate our minds?

3 John 1:11

Do not be _____ of _____.

Revelation 22:5

There will be no more _____. God will give us _____.

7

Strange Communication— Psychic Power

Lesson Focus

The unknown of this present and future life—and life after death—can be intriguing, especially for teenagers. The desire to communicate with the other side about this life and death purports to offer proof that there is life after death and can lead to involvement with Ouija boards and seances. Our real desire for knowledge should come from the Spirit who leads us in seeking God and His ways. In Christ Jesus can be found all our needs and all knowledge.

Objectives

By the power of the Holy Spirit, the participants, through the study of God's Word, will

1. recognize the occultic and demonic dangers of seances and Ouija boards;

2. reject those activities forbidden by God and encourage others to reject communication with spirits;

3. find comfort in God's plan for their life here and for all eternity.

Activity	Time Suggested	Materials Needed
Prayer	5 minutes	None
Amazing Insight!	10 minutes	5 Scenarios from page 74
The History and Background	10 minutes	Copies of Resource Page 7A
Two Stories	15 minutes	Bibles, newsprint, markers, copies of Resource Page 7B
Some Final Questions	10 minutes	Copies of Resource Page 7B, Bibles
Final Things to Remember	5 minutes	None
Closing Prayer	5 minutes	None

Prayer (5 minutes)

Begin with a prayer: "Dear God, You have created everything that has been, that is now, and that will ever come. Forgive us for looking for life's answers in places other than in You and Your Word. Thank You for Your Word that guides us, directs us, and gives us Your truth. Be with us as we look at the dangers of Ouija boards and seances. Have Your Spirit fill us with the desire to seek after You and Your ways. Through Your Son Jesus Christ. Amen.

Amazing Insight! (10 minutes)

Tell the group that you can read them according to your psychic powers and that you would like to give them some information from the other world. Read the following statements (memorize them if possible for effect).

Someone in this room has now, or once had . . . a mother.

Someone in this room did not brush his teeth this morning.

Someone in this room has had a relative in her family die in the last 100 years

Someone in this room has felt lonely.

Someone in this room has wanted some answers in life.

After this opening, follow up with: "Today we are looking at psychic connections, especially seances and Ouija boards. Why would anyone be a part of either of these activities? (Possible answers might be curiosity, loneliness, or sadness over a lost relative.) What are some of the dark realms that offer answers? (Astrology, gurus, tarot cards, palm readers, horoscopes, etc.) Where do you like to go for answers to tough questions? (Parents, friends, teachers, pastor, youth director) How can God help you when you need answers? (In His Word, He gives us comfort and guidance.)"

The History and Background (10 minutes)

Pass out copies of Resource Page 7A on Ouija boards and seances to the students. Read the history of these activities as a group.

Optional History Review

Give the students a pop quiz on the history of Ouija boards and seances.

1. Which one is older? (Ouija boards)

2. Which one is called a game? (Ouija boards)

3. Which one is a moneymaker? (Both)

4. Which one was admitted to be a hoax by its creators? (Seances)

5. Which one invites spirits? (Both)

6. Which one can lead to demon possessions? (Both)

Two Stories (15 minutes)

Tell the students you are going to be looking at two stories from the New Testament that deal with seeking knowledge and communication with spirits. Have the students divide into two groups and assign each group a story to look up and read through. Give each group a large piece of butcher paper or newsprint along with markers for their assignment.

Group A will look up Matthew 4:1–10 and complete this assignment. Ask the students to identify the three key issues of this conflict and illustrate them in a creative way on the paper. (Some suggestions might be that we should seek knowledge from God, receive guidance from the Word, and place our devotion in God.)

Group B will look up Acts 16:16–18 and complete this assignment. Ask the students to identify at least four things that we can learn about spirits from this encounter. (They are real, they know who God is, God controls them, and they seek their own good.)

After the groups have finished, pass out Resource Page 7B. Allow each group to present their story and share their assignments with the group. Encourage the students to fill in the appropriate answers on their student sheets.

If you have a creative group that likes to act out stories, allow each group to create a skit or drama for each of the stories as part of the presentation of their assignment.

Some Final Questions (10 minutes)

Say something such as, "These two stories have shown us that we can turn from demonic activity and seek God's wisdom in His Word. Let's see if there are other places in Scripture that can direct us. Look at the questions on your student page and we'll look up the corresponding passages."

Can we communicate with the dead? Luke 16:26 (There is a gap between life and death that can't be crossed.)

Then who is doing the communicating? 1 Peter 5:8 (The devil and demons)

How do we know the difference between good and bad spirits? 1 John 4:1–4 (There is one Holy Spirit who leads us to Jesus and completely follows the message of Scripture.)

What can happen if you get involved in these activities? 1 Timothy 4:1 (People may be deceived to follow the devil's spirits.)

What promise does God give in 1 John 4:4? (God is greater than Satan and has defeated all evil.)

What does God give us the power to do? James 4:7 (Resist the devil, and he will flee.)

So where do we go for answers? Proverbs 3:5–7 (By God's Spirit put your trust in and look to Him who through Christ has defeated the devil and all his ways.)

What does Colossians 2:16–20 say about worldly superstitions (even bad luck)? (They have no power and mean nothing in comparison to Christ.)

Final Things to Remember (5 minutes)

Conclude with these key points. You might want to have them printed on a board or newsprint.

Evil spirits are real and dangerous (1 Peter 5:8).

Jesus has control over life and death (Revelation 1:18).

God created everything and has power over it (Psalm 145:13).

God's Spirit gives us the knowledge we need (Colossians 1:9).

Closing Prayer (5 minutes)

Close with a prayer: "Dear heavenly Father, Creator of this world and Ruler over life and death. Through the death of Your Son, Jesus Christ, You conquered the evil one and all his demons. Forgive us for looking to all the wrong places for answers to things we should not know. Help us to be content with the vital information that is found only in You. Give us Your Holy Spirit to resist the devil and all his works and all his ways. Give us Your light to shine in the darkness of this fallen world. Through Your shining Son, Jesus, we pray. Amen."

Resources

Dale A. Meyer, *Matthew*, Lifelight Series (St. Louis: Concordia Publishing House, 1990)

Stoker Hunt, *Ouija, The Most Dangerous Game* (New York: Barnes and Noble Books, 1985)

Psychic Power: Ouija Board and Seances Fact Sheet

Ouija comes from combining the French word for yes, *oui,* and the German word for yes, *ja.* The word ouija means "yes, yes." Some traditions of occult hold that demons can't operate in a person's life uninvited. So ouija might be an invitation for spirits to connect with you. Christians are told in absolute terms to avoid all forms of evil, even if they appear harmless.

The earliest form of the Ouija board was found in ancient Chinese ruins from 500 B.C. The more recent version was invented in 1889 by Elihah Bond and bought by William Fuld in 1892. Fuld patented it and started the Baltimore Talking Board Co. Ouija were popular in World Wars I and II. By 1920 over three million boards were sold. The IRS took the makers to court, saying that it was a game and should be taxed. But lawyer Alen Fisher said that it was a medium for communication between this world and the spiritual realm. The IRS won the case; and it was the IRS who first called the Ouija board a game. However, the makers continued to see its spiritual involvement and never intended it to be a game.

The board consists of the alphabet, yes/no indicators, numbers zero through nine, and "good-bye." A three-legged platform called a *planchette* is passed over the board by participants. The planchette stops on letters, numbers, or words to spell or give messages.

The 1960s saw a rise in spiritualism and the Ouija again became popular. In 1966 Parker Brothers bought the rights and sold over two million copies. The Ouija board outsold Monopoly that year, and for a time, it was Parker Brothers' most popular game.

Christians believe that the Ouija board is not a game. Christians call upon God in prayer. The use of the Ouija board is completely different. It calls upon a power other than God. The only power other than God is Satan. Satan can communicate with us through these means. Yes, people can fake a message—and may often do so. However this does not mean that the devil, if invited, cannot enter into our thought process in this way. Those who study psychic phenomena see its dangers. Reports have shown that this is a tool of danger, and numerous cases of demon possession have occurred for those who are involved with Ouija boards.

Seances can be traced back to sisters Katie, Margaretta, and Leah Fox of New York who became famous in 1848 for conversing with a ghost who made loud rapping and popping noises. So many people came to see the Fox

sisters that they became world famous for their encounters with spirits. In 1888 Margaretta admitted it was a hoax and that she had made the sounds by popping her knee and toe joints.

Famous mediums have come forward to expose the secrets behind seances—using broad general statements that can mean a variety of things, eavesdropping, or doing research ahead of time about participants. Harry Houdini dabbled in the spiritual world apart from God and was haunted by the notion that someone might communicate with the dead. It nearly drove him insane—even though during his lifetime he was successful at debunking many mediums.

Modern-day seances are lead by psychics and mediums who are paid to communicate with the dead. Departed loved ones are invited to interact with the people present. Once again these communications with the other world open up participants to demonic possession and danger.

Page

7A

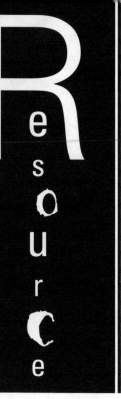

Ouija Boards / Seances

Ouija Boards and seances are both seen as tools to communicate with the other world, specifically the dead. However, they are actually tools of the devil used to deceive and lure people into seeking answers in the wrong places. People look all over for answers they want to know. Peace comes from the promise of Christ that helps us trust the message of God's Word. Think about that as you look into what the Bible has to say about these issues.

Two Stories

Group A   **Matt 4:1–10**
What are the three key issues in this conflict?

Group B   **Acts 16:16–18**
What are at least four things we can learn about spirits?

Some Final Questions

Can we communicate with the dead? **Luke 16:26**

Who is doing the communicating? **1 Peter 5:8**

How can we know the difference between good and bad spirits? **1 John 4:1–4**

What can happen if you get involved in these activities? **1 Timothy 4:1**

What promise does God give in **1 John 4:4**?

What does God give us the power to do? **James 4:7**

Where do we go for answers? **Proverbs 3:5–7**

What does **Colossians 2:16–20** say about worldly superstitions (even bad luck)?

8

Otherworldly Forces

Lesson Focus

The popular media creates great stories in the world of science fiction. Christian people may be entertained by sci-fi and even curious about the possibility of extraterrestrial life. While the popular media may lead us to believe that we are surrounded by aliens from other galaxies, the Scriptures do not directly address the subject. God's Word does, however, remind us that we are God's chosen people.

Objectives

By the power of the Holy Spirit, the participants, through the study of God's Word, will

1. understand the possibility of unhealthy interests in some science fiction and UFOs;

2. recognize that extreme interest in UFOs can lead to dangerous New Age religions, obsession with signs and Satan's kingdom, or agnostic denial of truth;

3. reject destructive and self-serving interests in science "cults";

4. rejoice in God's grace and truth, which He reveals through the mystery of the Gospel.

Lesson 8 Outline:

Activity	Time Suggested	Materials Needed
Prayer	3 minutes	None
Icebreaker Discussion	10 minutes	None
Introducing the Mystery	5 minutes	Copies of Resource Page 8A
Three Different Kinds of Mystery	15 minutes	Copies of Resource Page 8A
God's Mystery Revealed in Jesus Christ	25 minutes	Copies of Resource Page 8B, Bibles
Closing Prayer	5 minutes	None

Prayer (3 minutes)

"Heavenly Father, You are the Creator of the universe and the Source of all truth. You gave us Your written Word, the Bible, so that we can learn more about You and about how You love and guide us. Instead of hiding from us, You revealed Yourself to us in Your Son, Jesus, to help us know Your heart and mind. Send Your Holy Spirit now to open our eyes to the mystery of Your Gospel revealed in Jesus Christ. Forgive us for our errors, our foolish attempts at self-sufficiency, and all other sins. Keep us from chasing after spiritual fads or scientifically speculative dead ends. Give us discerning minds and help us to know and live in Your grace. We pray these things in the name of Your Son, Jesus. Amen."

Icebreaker Discussion (10 minutes)

Use the activities/questions below as an icebreaker exercise to help group members feel more at ease. Feel free to modify any of the discussion questions to suit the needs of your group.

Create a list of the top 10 most popular science fiction influences that touch young people's lives.

Why are people drawn to stories about science fiction, UFOs, and extraterrestrial life?

On one popular show, *The X-Files*, the FBI agents never give up on their investigations because they know that "the truth is out there." Does their search matter? Although it may be intriguing to watch, there are hidden dangers for some. When we investigate God's files, the Bible, we find the truth in Jesus. Is this important? You bet! In fact, this is a matter of life and death!

Introducing the Mystery (5 minutes)

Distribute copies of Resource Page 8A to support your discussion of the different ways that people might take science fiction seriously. Start the discussion with a couple of questions:

Many people are skeptical about whether or not extraterrestrial life even exists. However, some people take science fiction very seriously. Why do you think people become interested in UFOs?

Do you personally know anyone who thinks that UFOs are significant? If so, why do they think UFOs are important?

Some people are deeply influenced by "the Force," mind melds, and other elements of science fiction. How do you know if your interest has crossed the line?

Three Different Kinds of Mystery (15 minutes)

Some people take science fiction very seriously, and in starkly different ways.

Extraterrestrial Life: A New Age?

Some New Age religions teach that people can make themselves perfect and powerful. Sometimes they even promise superhuman abilities and immortal life. Not all, but some forms of science fiction promote unlimited human potential. This form of religious self-improvement is really an attempt to earn salvation by works. If we live our lives based on these ideas, we may have stepped into idolatry. Some people let their ideas become a religion, anticipating an extraterrestrial being who will come (via UFO) to grant perfection and power to those who are worthy in terms of religious practice. However, becoming worthy is simply another form of religious self-improvement, or salvation by works. These religions cannot show us people who measure up, or who have become perfect, because everyone sins. Some religions claim that extraterrestrial beings (who use UFOs to visit Earth) are examples of perfected people. These religions are dangerous! A few years ago the Heaven's Gate cult, for example, taught that a UFO would come to take their members to heaven. At least 39 of these people committed suicide, apparently under the direction of the cult leaders.

Reality check:

People cannot make themselves perfect; only God's grace in and through the death and resurrection of Jesus can rescue people from their weakness and sin. Any religion that counts on science or human potential is a dead end.

UFOs: End of the World?

A few groups of Christians associate UFOs with fallen angels who follow Satan and work his schemes in this world. Some of these groups try to correlate the appearance of UFOs with Bible texts (e.g., parts of Revelation) and see UFOs as an omen of the second coming of Christ. Obsession with signs and prophecies can get in the way of Christian growth, divert people from God's grace, and siphon off a tremendous amount of time and energy. The early church in Thessalonica encountered a similar problem when some of the members became preoccupied with the second coming of Christ. They even quit their jobs so that they could put more time into preparing for the end of time. Paul admonished them to quit being busybodies (1 Thessalonians

4:11–12) and to get back to work; his advice still holds for us today.

Reality check:

God encourages and enables us to keep our focus on Jesus Christ, the author of our salvation, rather than putting our time and energy into predicting the future or seeing signs of extraterrestrial life.

Conspiracy Theories? (Everyone Loves a Conspiracy!)

Some people believe that the government is hiding secrets about scientific advances, UFOs, and extraterrestrial beings. The lack of real evidence just confirms their suspicion that the government is hiding something. In a sense, this inability to know the truth turns people into agnostics who cannot seek truth ("It's futile!") or accept it if it is found ("Who can know?"). Scientific investigations have been able to explain many mysteries on the basis of geophysical and meteorological phenomena, but not all of them. However, some of the conspiracy theories have become so ridiculous that most reputable scientists are reluctant to work in this area. Thus, the conspiracy theories become almost self-fulfilling because they discourage credible research into scientific phenomena. Obsession with science fiction, UFOs, or any mystery becomes idolatry, leading the person away from fear, love, and trust in God above all things.

Reality check:

This kind of search is pointless. God is the author of truth and grants understanding to His children through Jesus Christ. The Scriptures proclaim the truth of God and eternal life through faith in Jesus Christ alone.

Sometimes people will point to Ezekiel's vision of a wheel (Ezekiel 1 and 10) as examples of UFOs in Scripture. Ezekiel's vision seems to indicate the complete mobility, or omniscience, of God and His power, so this should not be allowed to become a diversion in the discussion.

God's Mystery Revealed in Jesus Christ (25 minutes)

Distribute copies of Resource Page 8B. Lead the group through the Bible study to examine God's grace revealed in Jesus Christ. Emphasize God's revelation of the mystery of the Gospel to all humanity. His grace is a gift that is never discovered or earned through a self-improvement program.

His grace centers in Jesus Christ—not in signs, wonders, or attempts to analyze God's timetable. God created the world, including all scientific principles and possibilities. Science is created and not to be worshiped. Finally, God's revelation of the Gospel is tangible and real. Since it comes from God and not from man, it trumps anything that human study or religion could ever produce. We do not need to wonder or doubt if the truth might be clouded by human conspiracy.

Ephesians 3:1–12

Find each use of "mystery" in this passage. What was this "mystery of Christ" that became the focus of Paul's preaching? (The Gentiles are included as recipients of God's grace and salvation through Christ.)

How long had humanity waited for this mystery to be revealed? (Since the fall into sin)

How did Paul learn about this mystery and its meaning? How was the mystery of Christ revealed? (It was revealed by the Holy Spirit, through the work of the apostles and prophets.)

Which do you think is superior, God's wisdom or the "authorities in the heavenly realms" mentioned in 3:10? (Answers will vary.)

Colossians 1:25–29

Find each use of "mystery" in this passage. How long had the mystery been hidden? (For ages and generations)

To whom was the mystery revealed, and how was it revealed? (It was revealed to the saints, by the Spirit, through Paul.)

What is the purpose of Christ living in us? Compare this with the self-improvement goals of the New Age religions. (The indwelling of Christ strengthens us in our walk with Him.)

What can you conclude from these two passages (Ephesians and Colossians) regarding the content of God's mystery and the role of Jesus Christ in fulfilling it? (Christ is the key; it is only through faith in Christ that we gain eternal life.)

Did anyone have to discover or solve God's mystery on his or her own? Why or why not? (No, He reveals Himself through the power of the Holy Spirit.)

What is the role of God's grace in this mystery? (We rely solely on the grace of God.)

Closing Prayer (5 minutes)

Some members of your class may be struggling with their personal views about science fiction, especially UFOs. Some may have friends who have been led into one of the traps described on the fact sheet. Remember: All science fiction is not wrong—but our use of it or attitude toward it may be spiritually deadly. As you dismiss the class, consider meeting individually with those deeply involved in science fiction for further discussion, prayer, study, and counseling as appropriate.

Close in prayer: "Heavenly Father, people waited for Your salvation from the time of Adam and Eve until the arrival of Your Son, Jesus Christ. Thank You for Your grace in revealing the mystery of the Gospel through Your Word so that we may proclaim it to others. Give us Your wisdom and discernment. Keep us safe from risky diversions such as religious belief in science fiction, UFOs, obsessions with signs and evil powers, and fears of conspiracies. Help us instead to rejoice in Your grace that is ours in Jesus Christ. We pray these things in His name. Amen."

Resources

Further information about UFOs is available on the Web through any of the major search engines. However, people often post material on Web pages without any quality control or independent verification, and this kind of information may be incomplete or one-sided. Therefore, be careful about what you find on the Web unless you know its source!

👁 **http://www.junkscience.com/news2/ufo.htm**

📖 **http://www.lcms.org/cic** The Web address for the LCMS Church Information Center.

📖 **http://www.lcms.org/ctcr/coo.html** The Web address for the LCMS Commission on Organizations.

👁 **http://www.religioustolerance.org/**

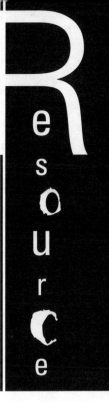

Three Different Kinds of Mystery

Many people doubt that extraterrestrial life exists. However, some people take science fiction very seriously and in starkly different ways.

Extraterrestrial Life: A New Age?

Some New Age religions teach that people can make themselves perfect and powerful. Sometimes they even promise superhuman abilities and immortal life. Not all, but some forms of science fiction promote unlimited human potential. This form of religious self-improvement is really an attempt to earn salvation by works. If we live our lives based on these ideas, we may have stepped into idolatry. Some people let these ideas become a religion, anticipating an extraterrestrial being who will come (via UFO) to grant perfection and power to those who are worthy in terms of religious practice. However, becoming worthy is simply another form of religious self-improvement, or salvation by works. These religions cannot show us people who measure up, or who have become perfect, because everyone sins. Some religions claim that extraterrestrial beings (who use UFOs to visit Earth) are examples of perfected people. These religions are dangerous! A few years ago the Heaven's Gate cult, for example, taught that a UFO would come to take their members to heaven. At least 39 of these people committed suicide, apparently under the direction of the cult leaders.

Reality check:

People cannot make themselves perfect; only God's grace in and through the death and resurrection of Jesus can rescue people from their weakness and sin. Any religion that counts on science or human potential is a dead end.

UFOs: End of the World?

A few groups of Christians associate UFOs with fallen angels who follow Satan and work his schemes in this world. Some of these groups try to correlate the appearance of UFOs with Bible texts (e.g., parts of Revelation) and see UFOs as an omen of the second coming of Christ. These groups mean well, but speculation about signs and omens can get in the way of the Gospel and distract from God's grace.

<u>Reality check</u>:

God encourages and enables us to keep our focus on Jesus Christ, the author of our salvation, rather than putting our time and energy into predicting the future or seeing signs of extraterrestrial life.

Conspiracy Theories?

Some people believe that the government is hiding secrets about scientific advances, UFOs, and extraterrestrial beings. The lack of real evidence just confirms their suspicion that the government is hiding something. In a sense, this inability to know the truth turns people into agnostics who cannot seek truth ("It's futile!") or accept it if it is found ("Who can know?").

<u>Reality check</u>:

We should recall that God is the author of truth and that He grants understanding through Jesus Christ. The Scriptures proclaim the truth of God and eternal life through Jesus Christ alone.

God's Mystery Revealed in Jesus Christ

People who investigate UFOs may never solve the mysteries of what cause the phenomenon or what UFOs mean. However, the Bible speaks of a much bigger mystery that means life or death for every person in the world. God authored this mystery, and people had to wait thousands of years for its solution. None of the claims of New Age religions, predictions of end-time signs and wonders, or supposed conspiracies come anywhere close to the significance and impact of God's mystery. The apostle Paul calls this "the mystery of the Gospel." Let's take a look at how God revealed His mystery and what it means for us.

Read Ephesians 3:1–12

Find each use of "mystery" in this passage. What was this "mystery of Christ" that became the focus of Paul's preaching? Summarize it in your own words.

How long had humanity waited for this mystery to be revealed?

Page

8B

How did Paul learn about this mystery and its meaning? How was the mystery of Christ revealed?

Which do you think is superior, God's wisdom or the "authorities in the heavenly realms" mentioned in **Ephesians 3:10**?

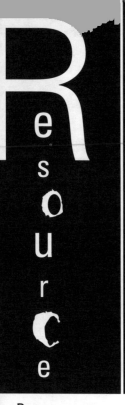

Read Colossians 1:25–29

Find each use of "mystery" in this passage. How long had the mystery been hidden?

To whom was the mystery revealed, and how was it revealed?

What is the purpose of Christ living in us? Compare this with the self-improvement goals of the New Age religions.

What can you conclude from these two passages (Ephesians and Colossians) regarding the content of God's mystery and the role of Jesus Christ in fulfilling it?

Did anyone have to discover or solve God's mystery on his or her own? Why or why not?

What is the role of God's grace in this mystery?

agnostic—someone who does not believe that the ultimate deity is identifiable; they do not believe in the existence or nonexistence of a god.

Agora—in Bible times, the marketplace where the people would meet to exchange merchandise, information, and ideas. See Acts 17:17.

astrology—the study of the planets and stars in an attempt to predict the events of one's life.

breakout groups—a small group of three to five students.

Colossae—a city in Phrygia, to whom Paul wrote the book of Colossians.

coven—a group of witches, usually totaling 13.

cult—a religion that is considered unorthodox, requiring extreme devotion from its followers.

dabbling—experimenting with, not fully involved.

deities—things that are ranked as godlike, revered as good and powerful.

desensitizer—something that causes one to become callous or insensitive toward something else.

doctrine—formal principles or statements of belief.

Druids—ancient Celtic priesthood founded in Great Britain.

Dungeons and Dragons—a fantasy game where participants assume roles in the game.

enlightenment—a philosophical movement of the eighteenth century that rejected traditional beliefs; or a state marked by the absence of desire or suffering.

extraterrestrial—originating outside of the earth or atmosphere.

folk religion—traditional religion of people from the same geographic location.

God—the triune God, Father, Son, and Holy Spirit.

gods—any number of false gods, not the true God.

Gospel—the message of salvation through faith in Jesus Christ. Also refers to the first four books of the New Testament.

grace—a free, unearned gift.

guru—a personal religious teacher.

Luther, Martin—Protestant reformer and founder of the Lutheran church.

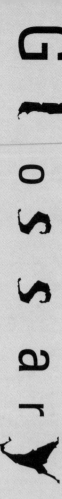

magick—the forbidden art of attempting to call upon spirit power practiced by witches.

medium—a person who conducts a seance and claims to communicate with the dead.

movement—an organized effort to promote a specific belief.

mysticism—the belief that spiritual truth can be gained through subjective experience.

New Age—late twentieth century system of beliefs based on Eastern and American-Indian traditions.

occult—matters influenced by the supernatural or supernormal.

occultic—related to or influenced by the occult.

Ouija board—a board that contains letters, numbers, yes/no indicators, and a pointer, or planchette. Users seeking answers to questions call on unseen powers to manipulate the pointer and board.

pagan—any number of non-Christian beliefs.

possessed—to be under the control of an unseen power, usually demonic.

practices—the actions of believers in a specific religion.

reincarnation—the belief that the soul is reborn and returns to earth after death as another person or animal.

religion—an organized group of persons who share the same beliefs.

ritual—a specific ceremony or action.

salvation—deliverance from the power of sin.

satanism—the formal worship of Satan.

shamanistic—related to the practice of religion by indigenous people, often involving magical powers.

spirituality—the quality of relating emotionally to matters of the spirit.

tarot cards—a set of 78 cards used in fortune-telling.

transcendence—the quality of rising above and beyond the limits.

transformation—to be completely changed.

UFO—unidentified flying object, related to anything unknown from other planets.

vampire—a person that is thought to come back from the dead to drink the blood of live victims.

voodoo—any number of folk religions that emphasize ancestor worship in order to gain power or insight.

werewolves—a person capable of assuming a wolf's form.

Wicca—Old English term for witch.

worldview—how a specific group sees the world.